D1391782

ROMEO AND JULIET

BY DAVID GARRICK

1750

A FACSIMILE PUBLISHED BY CORNMARKET PRESS
FROM THE COPY IN THE BIRMINGHAM SHAKESPEARE LIBRARY
LONDON
1969

PUBLISHED BY CORNMARKET PRESS LIMITED
42/43 CONDUIT STREET LONDON W1R ONL
PRINTED IN ENGLAND BY FLETCHER AND SON LIMITED NORWICH

SBN 7191 0175 1

ROMEO

AND

JULIET.

By SHAKESPEAR.

With ALTERATIONS, and an additional
SCENE:

As it is Performed at the *Theatre-Royal*
in *Drury-Lane*.

LONDON:
Printed for J. and R. TONSON and S. DRAPER,
MDCCL.

September 29, 1750.

Advertisement.

*THE Alterations in the following Play
are few, except in the last act; the
Design was to clear the Original as much
as possible, from the Jingle and Quibble
which were always thought a great Ob-
jection to performing it.*

*When this Play was reviv'd two Win-
ters ago, it was generally thought, that
the sudden Change of* Romeo's *Love from*
Rosaline *to* Juliet *was a Blemish in his
Character, and therefore it is to be hop'd
that an Alteration in that Particular will
be excus'd; the only Merit that is claim'd
from it is, that it is done with as little
Injury to the Original as possible.*

David Garrick.

Drama-

Dramatis Personæ.

ROMEO,	Mr. *Garrick.*
Eſcalus,	Mr. *Winſtone.*
Paris,	Mr. *Lee.*
Mountague,	Mr. *Burton.*
Capulet,	Mr. *Berry.*
Mercutio,	Mr. *Woodward.*
Benvolio,	Mr. *Mozeen.*
Tibalt,	Mr. *Blakes.*
Old Capulet,	Mr. *Wright.*
Friar Lawrence,	Mr. *Havard.*
Friar John,	Mr. *Paddick.*
Balthaſar,	Mr. *Ackman.*
Gregory,	Mr. *W.Vaughan.*
Sampſon,	Mr. *James.*
Abram,	Mr. *Marr.*
JULIET,	Miſs *Bellamy.*
Lady Capulet,	Mrs. *Bennet.*
Nurſe,	Mrs. *James.*

Citizens of Verona, *ſeveral men and women relations to* Capulet, *Maskers, guards and other Attendants.*

The SCENE, *in the beginning of the fifth act, is in* Mantua; *during all the reſt of the Play, in and near* Verona.

ROMEO

ROMEO and JULIET.

A C T I. S C E N E I.

The Street in Verona.

Enter Sampson *and* Gregory.

SAMPSON.

*G*REGORY, I strike quickly, being mov'd.

Greg. But thou art not quickly mov'd to strike.

Sam. A dog of the house of *Mountague* moves me.

Greg. Draw thy tool then, for here come of that house.

Enter Abram *and* Balthasar.

Sam. My naked weapon is out; Quarrel I will back thee, but——Let us take the law of our sides: let them begin.

Greg. I will frown as I pass by, and let them take it as they list.

Sam. Nay as they dare. I will bite my thumb at them, which is a disgrace to them, if they bear it.

Abr. Do you bite your thumb at us, Sir?

Sam. I do bite my thumb, Sir.

Abr. Do you bite your thumb at us, Sir?

Sam. Is the law on our side, if I say ay?

A 4

Greg.

Greg. No.

Sam. No, Sir, I do not bite my thumb at you, Sir : but I bite my thumb, Sir.

Greg. Do you quarrel, Sir ?

Abr. Quarrel, Sir ? no, Sir.

Sam. If you do, Sir, I am for you : I ſerve as good a man as you.

Abr. No better, Sir.

Sam. Well, Sir.

Enter Benvolio.

Greg. Say better : here comes one of my maſter's kinſmen.

Sam. Yes, better, Sir.

Abr. You lye.

Sam. Draw, if you be men. *Gregory*, remember thy ſwaſhing blow.   [*They fight.*

Ben. Part, fools, put up your ſwords, you know not what you do.

Enter Tibalt.

Tib. What, art thou drawn amongſt theſe heartleſs hinds ?

Turn thee, *Benvolio*, look upon thy death.

Ben. I do but keep the peace ; put up thy ſword, Or manage it to part theſe men with me.

Tib. What drawn, and talk of peace ? I hate the word As I hate hell, all *Mountagues* and thee : Have at thee, coward.   [*Fight.*

Enter three or four citizens with clubs.

Offi. Clubs, bills, and partiſans ! ſtrike ! beat them down.

Down with the *Capulets*, down with the *Mountagues.*

Enter old Capulet *in his Gown.*

Cap. What noiſe is this ? give me my ſword, My ſword, I ſay : old *Mountague* is come, And flouriſhes his blade in ſpite of me.

Enter old Mountague.

Moun. Thou villain, *Capulet*————Hold me not, let me go.

Enter Prince, with attendants.

Prin. Rebellious ſubjects, enemies to peace, Prophaners of your neighbour-ſtained ſteel————

Will they not hear ? what ho ! you men ! you beaſts,

                 That

That quench the fire of your pernicious rage,
With purple fountains issuing from your veins ;
On pain of torture, from those bloody hands
Throw your mis-temper'd weapons to the ground,
And hear the sentence of your moved prince.
Three civil broils, bred of an airy word,
By thee, old *Capulet*, and *Mountague*,
Have thrice disturb'd the quiet of our state.
If ever you affright our streets again,
Your lives shall pay the forfeit of the peace.
For this time all the rest depart away,
You, *Capulet*, shall go along with me ;
And *Mountague*, come you this afternoon,
To know our further pleasure.
Once more, on pain of death, all men depart.

[Exeunt Prince and Capulet.

S C E N E II.

Manent Mountague *and* Benvolio.

Moun. WHO set this antient quarrel new abroach?
Speak, nephew, were you by when it
began ?
Ben. Here were the servants of your adversary,
And yours, close fighting, ere I did approach ;
I drew to part them : In the instant came
The fiery *Tibalt*, with his sword prepar'd,
Which as he breath'd defiance to my ears,
He swung about his head, and cut the winds.
While we were interchanging thrusts and blows,
Came more and more, and fought on part and part,
'Till the Prince came.
Moun. O where is *Romeo ?*
Right glad am I, he was not at this fray.
Ben. My lord, an hour before the worshipp'd sun
Peep'd through the golden window of the East,
A troubled mind drew me to walk abroad ;
Where underneath the grove of sycamour,
That westward rooteth from this city side,
So early walking did I see your son.

A 5

Tow'rds

Tow'rds him I made, but he was 'ware of me,
And stole into the covert of the wood.
I measuring his affections by my own,
(That most are busied when they're most alone,)
Pursu'd my humour, not pursuing him,
And gladly shunn'd, who gladly fled from me.

Moun. Many a morning hath he there been seen
With tears augmenting the fresh morning dew ;
But all so soon as the all-chearing sun
Should, in the farthest east, begin to draw
The shady curtains from *Aurora*'s bed ;
Away from light steals home my heavy son,
And private in his chamber pens himself ;
Shuts up his windows, locks fair day-light out,
And makes himself an artificial night.
Black and portentous must this humour prove,
Unless good counsel may the cause remove.

Ben. My noble uncle, do you know the cause ?

Moun. I neither know it, nor can learn it of him.

Ben. Have you importun'd him by any means ?

Moun. Both by myself and many other friends ;
But he, his own affection's counsellor,
Is to himself (I will not say how true)
But to himself so secret and so close.
So far from sounding and discovery ;
As is the bud bit with an envious worm,
Ere he can spread his sweet leaves to the air,
Or dedicate his beauty to the sun.

Ben. So please you, Sir, *Mercutio* and myself
Are most near to him ; be't that our years,
Statures, births fortunes, studies, inclinations,
Measure the rule of his, I know not ; but
Friendship still loves to sort him with his like.
We will attempt upon his privacy,
And could we learn from whence his sorrows grow,
We would as willingly give cure, as knowledge.

Moun. 'Twill bind us to you : good *Benvolio*, go.

Ben. We'll know his grievance, or be hard denied.

[*Exeunt severally.*

SCENE

S C E N E   III.

Before Capulet's *House.*

Enter Capulet *and* Paris.

Cap. AND *Mountague* is bound as well as I,
In penalty alike ; and 'tis not hard
For men so old as we to keep the peace.
Par. Of honourable reck'ning are you both,
And pity 'tis you liv'd at odds so long :
But now, my lord, what say you to my suit ?
Cap. But saying o'er what I have said before,
My child is yet a stranger in the world,
She hath not seen the change of eighteen years ;
Let two more summers wither in their pride,
Ere we may think her ripe to be a wife.
Par. Younger than she are happy mothers made.
Cap. And too soon marr'd are those so early made :
The earth hath swallow'd all my hopes but her.
But woo her, gentle *Paris*, get her will,
Fortune to her consent is but a part ;
If she agree, within her scope of choice
Lies my consent ; so woo her gentle *Paris.*
This night I hold an old accustom'd feast,
Whereto I have invited many a friend,
Such as I love, and you among the rest ;
One more most welcome ! Come, go in with me.
[*Exeunt.*

S C E N E   IV.

A Wood near Verona.

Enter Benvolio *and* Mercutio.

Mer. SEE where he steals—Told I you not, *Benvolio,*
That we should find this melancholy *Cupid*
Lock'd in some gloomy covert, under key
Of cautionary silence ; with his arms
Threaded, like these cross boughs, in sorrow's knot.
Enter

Enter ROMEO.

Ben. Good morrow, Coufin.

Rom. Is the day fo young?

Ben. But now ſtruck nine.

Rom. Ah me! ſad hours feem long.

Mer. Prithee: what ſadneſs lengthens *Romeo*'s hours?

Rom. Not having that, which having makes them ſhort.

Ben. In love, me ſeems!

Alas, that love fo gentle to the view,

Should be fo tyrannous and rough in proof!

Rom. Where ſhall we dine?—O me—Couſin *Benvolio,*

What was the fray this morning with the *Capulets?*

Yet, tell me not, for I have heard it all.

Here's much to do with hate, but more with love:

Love, heavy lightneſs! ferious vanity!

Miſ-ſhapen chaos of well-ſeeming forms!

This love feel I; but ſuch my froward fate,

That there I love where moſt I ought to hate.

Doſt thou not laugh, my couſin? Oh *Juliet, Juliet!*

Ben. No, coz, I rather weep.

Rom. Good heart, at what?———

Ben. At thy good heart's oppreſſion.

Mer. Tell me in ſadneſs, who ſhe is you love?

Rom. In ſadneſs then, I love a woman.

Mer. I aim'd fo near, when I ſuppos'd you lov'd.

Rom. A right good markſman! and ſhe's fair I love:

But knows not of my love, 'twas thro' my eyes

The ſhaft empierc'd my heart, chance gave the wound,

Which time can never heal: no ſtar befriends me,

To each ſad night ſucceeds a diſmal morrow,

And ſtill 'tis hopeleſs love, and endleſs ſorrow.

Mer. Be rul'd by me, forget to think of her.

Rom. O teach me how I ſhould forget to think

Mer. By giving liberty unto thine eyes:

Take thou ſome new infection to thy heart,

And the rank poiſon of the old will die.

Examine other beauties.

Rom. He that is ſtrucken blind cannot forget

The precious treaſure of his eye-ſight loſt.

Shew me a miſtreſs that is paſſing fair;

What doth her beauty ſerve but as a note,

Remembring

Remembring me, who paſt that paſſing fair ;
Farewel, thou canſt not teach me to forget.

Mer. I warrant thee. If thou'lt but ſtay to hear,
To night there is an ancient ſplendid feaſt
Kept by old *Capulet,* our enemy,
Where all the beauties of *Verona* meet.

Rom. At *Capulet*'s !

Mer. At *Capulet*'s, my friend,
Go there, and with an unattainted eye,
Compare her face with ſome that I ſhall ſhow,
And I will make thee think thy ſwan a raven.

Rom. When the devout religion of mine eye
Maintains ſuch falſhoods, then turn tears to fires ;
And burn the hereticks. All-ſeeing Phœbus
Ne'er ſaw her match, ſince firſt his courſe began.

Ben. Tut, tut, you ſaw her fair, none elſe being by,
Herſelf pois'd with herſelf ; but let be weigh'd
Your lady's love againſt ſome other fair,
And ſhe will ſhew ſcant well.

Rom. I will along, *Mercutio.*

Mer. 'Tis well. Look to behold at this high feaſt,
Earth-treading ſtars, that make dim heaven's lights.
Hear all, all ſee, try all ; and like her moſt,
That moſt ſhall merit thee.

Rom. My mind is chang'd ———
I will not go to night.

Mer. Why, may one ask ?

Rom. I dream'd a dream laſt night.

Mer. Ha ! ha ! a dream !
O then I ſee queen Mab hath been with you.
She is the fancy's mid-wife, and ſhe comes
In ſhape no bigger than an agat-ſtone
On the fore-finger of an Alderman,
Drawn with a team of little atomies,
Athwart mens noſes as they lie aſleep :
Her waggon-ſpokes made of long ſpinners legs ;
The cover, of the wings of graſhoppers ;
The traces, of the ſmalleſt ſpider's web ;
The collars, of the moonſhine's watry beams ;
Her whip, of cricket's bone ; the laſh, of film ;
Her waggoner a ſmall gray-coated gnat,
Not half ſo big as a round little worm,

Prick'd

Prick'd from the lazy finger of a maid.
Her chariot is an empty hazel-nut,
Made by the joiner squirrel, or old grub,
Time out of mind the fairies coach-makers :
And in this state she gallops night by night,
Through lovers brains, and then they dream of love;
On courtiers knees, that dream on curtsies straight :
O'er lawyers fingers, who straight dream on fees :
O'er ladies lips, who straight on kisses dream,
Sometimes she gallops o'er a lawyer's nose,
And then dreams he of smelling out a suit :
And sometimes comes she with a tith-pig's tail,
Tickling the Parson as he lies asleep ;
Then dreams he of another benefice.
Sometimes she driveth o'er a soldier's neck,
And then dreams he of cutting foreign throats,
Of breaches, ambuscadoes, *Spanish* blades,
Of healths five fathom deep ; and then anon
Drums in his ears, at which he starts and wakes,
And being thus frighted, swears a prayer or two,
And sleeps again. This is that *Mab* ————

   Rom. Peace, peace, *Mercutio,* peace :
Thou talk'st of nothing.

   Mer. True, I talk of dreams ;
Which are the children of an idle brain,
Begot of nothing, but vain phantasy,
Which is as thin of substance as the air,
And more unconstant than the wind.

   Ben. This wind you talk of, blows us from ourselves,
And we shall come too late.

   Rom. I fear too early : for my mind misgives
Some consequence, still hanging in the stars,
From this night's revels.—lead, gallant friends ;
Let come what may, once more I will behold,
My *Juliet's* eyes, drink deeper of affliction :
I'll watch the time, and mask'd from observation
Make known my sufferings, but conceal my name :
Tho' hate and discord 'twixt our fires increase,
Let in our hearts dwell love and endless peace.
                [*Exeunt Mer. and Ben.*

SCENE

S C E N E V.

Capulet's *House.*

Enter Lady Capulet, *and Nurse.*

La. Cap. NURSE, where's my daughter? call her
forth to me.

Nurse. Now (by my maiden-head, at twelve year old)
I bad her come; what lamb, what lady-bird, God forbid——where's this girl? what, *Juliet?*

Enter Juliet.

Jul. How now, who calls?

Nurse. Your mother.

Jul. Madam, I am here, what is your will?

La. Cap. This is the matter——— Nurse, give leave
a while, we must talk in secret; Nurse, come back again,
I have remembred me, thou shalt hear my counsel: thou
know'st my daughter's of a pretty age.

Nurse. Faith I can tell her age unto an hour.

La. Cap. She's not eighteen.

Nurse. I'll lay eighteen of my teeth, and yet to my
teeth be it spoken, I have but eight, she's not eighteen;
how long is it now to *Lammas* tide?

La. Cap. A fortnight and odd Days.

Nurse. Even or odd, of all Days in the year come
Lammas-eve at night shall she be eighteen. *Susan* and
she (God rest all christian souls) were of an age. Well,
Susan is with God; she was too good for me. But as I
said, on *Lammas*-eve at night shall she be eighteen, that
shall she, marry, I remember it well. 'Tis since the
earthquake now fifteen Years, and she was wean'd; I never shall forget it, of all the Days in the year, upon that
day; for I had then laid wormwood to my breast, sitting
in the sun under the dove-house wall; my lord and you
were then at *Mantua* —— nay, I do bear a brain. But
as I said, when it did taste the wormwood on the nipple
of the breast, and felt it bitter, pretty fool, to see it teachy
and fall out with the breast. Shake, quoth the dove-
house—'twas no need I trow, to bid me trudge; and
since that time it is fifteen years, for then she could stand
alone, nay, by th' rood she could have run, and wad-
led

led all about; for even the day before she broke her brow;
and then my husband, (God be with his soul, a' was a
merry man,) took up the child ; yea quoth he, dost thou
fall upon thy face? thou wilt fall backward when thou hast
more wit; wilt thou not *Julé*? and by my holy dam, the
pretty wretch left crying, and said, ay ; To see now how
a jest shall come about I warrant, and I should live a thousand Years, I should not forget it : Wilt thou not, *Julé*,
quoth he ? and pretty fool, it stinted, and said, ay.

Jul. And stint thee too, I pray thee peace.

Nurse. Peace, I have done ; God mark thee to his grace,
Thou wast the prettiest babe that e'er I nurst :
And I might live to see thee married once,
I have my wish.

La. Cap. And that same marriage is the very theme
I came to talk of. Tell me, daughter *Juliet*,
How stands your disposition to be married ?

Jul. It is an honour that I dream not of.

Nurse. An honour ? were not I thine only nurse,
I'd say thou hadst suck'd wisdom from thy teat.

La. Cap. Well, think of marriage now; younger
        than you
Here in *Verona*, ladies of esteem,
Are made already mothers. By my 'count,
I was your mother much upon these years
That you are now a maid. Thus then in brief,
The valiant *Paris* seeks you for his love.

Nurse. A man, young lady, lady, such a man
As all the world —— Why he's a man of wax.

La. Cap. *Verona*'s summer hath not such a flower.

Nurse. Nay he's a flower, in faith a very flower.

La. Cap. Speak briefly, can you like of *Paris* love ?

Jul. I'll look to like, if looking liking move ;
But no more deep will I indart my eye,
Then your consent gives strength to make it fly.

Enter Gregory.

Greg. Madam, new guests are come, and brave ones,
all in masks. You are call'd; my young lady asked for,
the Nurse curs'd in the pantry; supper almost ready to
be serv'd up, and every thing in extremity. I must
hence and wait.

La. Cap. We follow thee.   [*Exeunt.*
                                          SCENE

S C E N E VI.

A Hall in Capulet's *House.*

The Capulets, *Ladies, Guests, and Maskers, are discover'd.*

Cap. WElcome, Gentlemen.   Ladies, that have
            your feet
Unplagued with corns, we'll have a bout with you.
Who'll now deny to dance? She that makes dainty,
I'll swear hath corns.   I have seen the day e'er now,
That I have worn a Visor, and cou'd tell
A whispering tale in a fair lady's ear,
Such as would please; 'tis gone; 'tis gone; 'tis gone!
                    [*Musick plays, and they dance.*
More light ye knaves, and turn the tables up ;
And quench the fire, the room is grown too hot.
Ah, Sirrah, this unlook'd-for sport comes well.
Nay sit, nay sit, good cousin *Capulet,*
For you and I are past our dancing days :
How long is't now since last yourself and I
Were in a mask ?

    2 Cap. By'r lady, thirty years.

    Cap. What, man! 'tis not so much, 'tis not so much ;
'Tis since the nuptial of *Lucentio,*
Come Pentecost as quickly as it will,
Some five and twenty years, and then we mask'd.

    2 Cap. 'Tis more, 'tis more ; his son is elder, Sir :
His son is thirty.

    Cap. Will you tell me that ?
His son was but a ward two years ago.

    Rom. Cousin *Benvolio,* do you mark that Lady, which
Doth enrich the hand of yonder gentleman.

    Ben. I do.

    Rom. Does she not teach the torches how to shine ? *to burn brig*
Her beauty hangs upon the cheek of night,
Like a rich jewel in an *Æthiops'* ear;
The measure done, I'll watch her to her place,
And touching hers, make happy my rude hand.
Be still, be still, my fluttering heart.

    Tib. This by his voice should be a *Mountague,*
Fetch me my rapier, boy ; what, dares the slave
Come hither cover'd with an antick face,   T*o*

To fleer and fcorn at our folemnity?
Now by the ftock and honour of my Race,
To ftrike him dead I hold it not a fin.

 Cap. Why, how now, kinfman, wherefore ftorm you
   thus?

 Tib. Uncle, this is a *Mountague*, our foe:
A villain that is hither come in fpite,
To fcorn and flout at our folemnity.

 Cap. Young *Romeo*, is't?

 Tib. That villain *Romeo*.

 Cap. Content thee, gentle coz, let him alone,
He bears him like a courtly gentleman:
And to fay truth, *Verona* brags of him,
To be a virtuous and well-govern'd youth.
I would not for the wealth of all this town
Here in my houfe do him difparagement:
Therefore be patient, take no note of him.

 Tib. It fits, when fuch a villain is a gueft.
I'll not endure him.

 Cap. He fhall be endur'd.
Be quiet, Coufin, or I'll make you quiet——

 Tib. Patience perforce with wilful choler **meeting,**
Makes my flefh tremble in their difference.
I will withdraw; but this intrufion fhall,
Now feeming fweet, convert to bitter gall.
          [*A Dance here.*

 Rom. If I prophane with my unworthy hand
             [*To Juliet.*
This holy fhrine, the gentle fine is this.   [*Kifs.*

 Jul. Good pilgrim, you do wrong your hand too
   much,
For palm to palm is holy palmer's kifs.

 Rom. Have not faints lips, and holy palmers too?

 Jul. Ay, pilgrim, lips that they muft ufe in prayer.

 Rom. Thus then, dear faint, let lips put up their prayers.
             [*Kifs.*

 Nurfe. Madam, your mother craves a word with you.

 Ben. What is her mother?   [*To her nurfe.*

 Nurfe. Marry, bachelor,
Her mother is the lady of the houfe,
And a good lady, and a wife and virtuous,
I nurs'd her daughter that you talk'd withal:

            I tell

I tell you, he that can lay hold on her
Shall have the chink.

Ben. Is she a *Capulet?*

Romeo, let's be gone, the sport is over.

Rom. Ay, so I fear, the more is my mishap. [*Ex.*

Cap. Nay, gentlemen, prepare not to be gone,
We have a trifling foolish banquet towards.|
Is it e'en so? why then, I thank you all.
I thank you, honest gentlemen, good night:
More torches here—come on, then let's to supper.
[*Exeunt.*

Jul. Come hither, nurse. What is yon gentleman?

Nurse. The son and heir of old *Tiberio*

Jul. What's he that is now going out of door?

Nurse. That, as I think, is young *Mercutio.*

Jul. What's he that follows here, that would not
dance?

Nurse. I know not.

Jul. Go ask his name. If he be married,
My grave is like to be my wedding-bed.

Nurse. His name is *Romeo,* and a *Mountague,*
The only son of your great enemy.

Jul. My only love sprung from my only hate!
Too early seen, unknown; and known too late.

Nurse. What's this? what's this?

Jul. A rhime I learn'd e'en now
Of one I talk'd withal.
[*One calls within,* Juliet.

Nurse. Anon, anon——
Come, let's away, the strangers are all gone. [*Exeunt.*

ACT

ACT II. SCENE I.

The STREET.

Enter Romeo *alone.*

ROMEO.

CAN I go forward when my heart is here?
  Turn back, dull earth, and find thy center out. [*Exit.*

Enter Benvolio *with* Mercutio.

Ben. Romeo, my coufin Romeo.

Mer. He is wife,
And on my life hath ftol'n him home to bed.

Ben. He ran this way, and leap'd this orchard wall,
Call, good *Mercutio.*

Mer. Nay, I'll conjure too.
Why, *Romeo!* humours! madman! paffion! lover!
Appear thou in the likenefs of a Sigh,
Speak but one Rhime, and I am fatisfied.
Cry but *Ah me!* couple but *love* and *dove,*
Speak to my goffip *Venus* one fair word,
One nick-name to her purblind fon and heir;
I conjure thee by thy miftrefs's bright eyes,   *Rosaline's*
By her high forehead, and her fcarlet lip,
By her fine foot, ftraight leg, and quivering thigh,
And the demeafns that there adjacent lie,
That in thy likenefs thou appear to us.

Ben. An if he hear thee, thou wilt anger him.

Mer. This cannot anger him: 'twould anger him
To raife a fpirit in his miftrefs' circle
'Till fhe had laid it.   My invocation is
Honeft and fair, and in his miftrefs' name,
I conjure only but to raife him up.

Ben. Come, he hath hid himfelf among thefe trees,
To be conforted with the hum'rous night.

Mer. Romeo, good night, I'll to my truckle bed,
This field-bed is too cold for me to fleep:
Come, fhall we go?

Ben. Go then, for 'tis in vain
To feek him here that means not to be found. [*Exeunt.*
SCENE

S C E N E II.
A G A R D E N.

Enter Romeo.

Rom. HE jefts at fcars that never felt a wound——
But foft, what light thro' yonder window
breaks ?
It is the eaft, and *Juliet* is the fun !
[Juliet *appears above at a window.*
Arife, fair fun, and kill the envious moon,
Who is already fick and pale with grief,
That thou, her maid, art far more fair than fhe.
She fpeaks, yet fhe fays nothing ; what of that ?
Her eye difcourfes, I will anfwer it ;
I am too bold—Oh were thofe eyes in heav'n,
They'd through the airy region ftream fo bright,
That birds would fing and think it were the morn :
See how fhe leans her cheek upon her hand !
O that I were a glove upon that hand,
That I might touch that cheek !
   Jul. Ah me !
   Rom. She fpeaks, fhe fpeaks !
Oh fpeak again, bright angel, for thou art
As glorious to this fight
As is a winged meffenger from heav'n,
To the upturn'd wondering eyes of mortals
When he beftrides the lazy-pacing clouds,
And fails upon the bofom of the air.
   Jul. O *Romeo*, *Romeo*—wherefore art thou *Romeo* ?
Deny thy father, and refufe thy name :
Or if thou wilt not, be but fworn my love,
And I'll no longer be a *Capulet.*
   Rom. Shall I hear more, or fhall I fpeak at this ?
                                        [*Afide.*
   Jul. 'Tis but thy name that is my enemy ;
Thou art not thyfelf fo, tho' a *Montague.*
What's in a name ? that which we call a rofe,
By any other name would fmell as fweet.
So *Romeo* would, were he not *Romeo* call'd,

                                        Retain

Retain that dear perfection which he owes,
Without that title; *Romeo,* quit thy name,
And for that name, which is no part of thee,
Take all myſelf.

 Rom. I take thee at thy word:
Call me but love, I will forſake my name,
And never more be *Romeo.*

 Jul. What man art thou, that thus beſcreen'd in night
So ſtumbleſt on my counſel?

 Rom. I know not how to tell thee who I am:
My name, dear ſaint, is hateful to myſelf,
Becauſe it is an enemy to thee.

 Jul. My ears have yet not drunk a hundred words
Of that tongue's uttering, yet I know the ſound.
Art thou not *Romeo,* and a *Montague?*

 Rom. Neither, fair ſaint, if either thee diſpleaſe.

 Jul. How cam'ſt thou hither, tell me, and for what?
The orchard-walls are high, and hard to climb,
And the place death, conſidering who thou art,
If any of my kinſmen find thee here.

 Rom. With love's light wings did I o'er-perch theſe
   walls,
For ſtony limits cannot hold love out,
And what love can do, that dares love attempt:
Therefore thy kinſmen are no ſtop to me.

 Jul. If they do ſee thee, they will murder thee.

 Rom. Alack, there lies more peril in thine eye,
Than twenty of their ſwords; look thou but ſweet,
And I am proof againſt their enmity.

 Jul. I would not for the world they ſaw thee here,
By whoſe direction found'ſt thou out this place?

 Rom. By love, that firſt did prompt me to enquire,
He lent me counſel, and I lent him eyes:
I am no pilot, yet wert thou as far
As that vaſt ſhore, waſh'd with the fartheſt ſea,
I would adventure for ſuch merchandiſe.

 Jul. Thou know'ſt the maſk of night is on my face,
Elſe would a maiden bluſh bepaint my cheek
For that which thou haſt heard me ſpeak to night.
Fain would I dwell on form, fain, fain deny
What I have ſpoke——but farewel compliment:
Doſt thou love me? I know thou wilt ſay, ay,

         And

And I will take thy word——yet if thou fwear'ft,
Thou may'ft prove falfe ; at lovers perjuries
They fay *Jove* laughs. Oh gentle *Romeo*,
If thou doft love, pronounce it faithfully :
Or if thou think I am too quickly won,
I'll frown and be perverfe, and fay thee nay,
So thou wilt woo : but elfe not for the world.
In truth, fair *Mountague*, I am too fond ;
And therefore thou may'ft think my 'haviour light :
But truft me, gentleman, I'll prove more true,
Than thofe that have more cunning to be ftrange.
I fhould have been more ftrange, I muft confefs,
But that thou over-heard'ft, ere I was ware,
My true love's paffion ; therefore pardon me,
And not impute this yielding to light love,
Which the dark night hath fo difcovered.

   Rom. Lady, by yonder bleffed moon I vow——
   Jul. O fwear not by the moon, th' inconftant moon,
That monthly changes in her circled orb ;
Left that thy love prove likewife variable.

   Rom. What fhall I fwear by ?
   Jul. Do not fwear at all ;
Or if thou wilt, fwear by thy gracious felf,
Which is the god of my idolatry,
And I'll believe thee.

   Rom. If my true heart's love——
   Jul. Well, do not fwear——although I joy in thee,
I have no joy of this contract to night ;
It is too rafh, too unadvis'd, too fudden ;
Too like the lightning which doth ceafe to be
Ere one can fay, it lightens—fweet, good night.
This bud of love by fummer's ripening breath
May prove a beauteous flower when next we meet :
Good night, good night—as fweet repofe and reft
Come to thy heart, as that within my breaft.

   Rom. O wilt thou leave me fo unfatisfied ?
   Jul. What fatisfaction canft thou have to-night ?
   Rom. Th' exchange of thy love's faithful vow for mine.
   Jul. I gave thee mine before thou didft requeft it :
And yet I would it were to give again.

   Rom. Wouldft thou withdraw it ? for what purpofe,
      love ?

                              Jul.

Jul. But to be frank, and give it thee again.
My bounty is as boundlefs as the fea,
My love as deep; the more I give to thee,
The more I have, for both are infinite.
I hear fome noife within; dear love, adieu.

                        [*Nurfe calls within*

Anon, good Nurfe——Sweet *Mountague*, be true;
Stay but a little, I will come again.   [*Exit.*
    Rom. O bleffed, bleffed night.   I am afraid
All this is but a dream! being in Night,
Too flattering fweet to be fubftantial.

            Re-enter Juliet *above.*

    Jul. Three words, dear *Romeo*, and good night indeed:
If that thy bent of love be honourable,
Thy purpofe marriage, fend me word to morrow,
By one that I'll procure to come to thee,
Where and what time thou wilt perform the rite;
And all my fortunes at thy foot I'll lay,
And follow thee, my love, throughout the world.

                    [*Within :* Madam.

I come, anon————but if thou mean'ft not well,
I do befeech thee——[*Within :* Madam.] By and by I
        come————
To ceafe thy fuit, and leave me to my grief.
To morrow will I fend.
    Rom. So thrive my foul.
    Jul. A thoufand times good night.   [*Exit.*
    Rom. A thoufand times the worfe to want thy light.

            Enter Juliet *again.*

    Jul. Hift! *Romeo*, hift! O for a falkner's voice,
To lure his Taffel gentle back again————
Bondage is hoarfe and may not fpeak aloud,
Elfe would I tear the cave where Echo lies,
And make her angry tongue more hoarfe than mine
With repetition of my *Romeo*.
    Rom. It is my love that calls upon my name.
How filver-fweet found lovers tongues by night,
Like foftest mufick to attending ears!
    Jul. Romeo!
    Rom. My fweet!
    Jul. At what a clock to-morrow
Shall I fend to thee?

                            Rom.

Rom. By the hour of nine.

Jul. I will not fail, 'tis twenty years 'till then,——
I have forgot why I did call thee back.

Rom. Let me ftand here 'till thou remember it.

Jul. I fhall forget to have thee ftill ftand there,
Remembring how I love thy Company.

Rom. And I'll ftay here, to have thee ftill forget,
Forgetting any other home but this.

Jul. 'Tis almoft morning. I would have thee gone,
And yet no further than a Wanton's bird,
That lets it hop a little from her hand,
And with a filk thread plucks it back again,
So loving jealous of his liberty.

Rom. I would I were thy bird.

Jul. Sweet, fo would I,
Yet I fhould kill thee with much cherifhing.
Good night, good night. Parting is fuch fweet forrow,
That I fhall fay good night 'till it be morrow.   [*Exit.*

Rom. Sleep dwell upon thine Eyes, peace in thy breaft;
Would I were fleep and peace, fo fweet to reft!
Hence will I to my ghoftly father's cell,
His help to crave, and my dear hap to tell.   [*Exit.*

S C E N E   III.

A Monaftery.

Enter Friar Lawrence *with a basket.*

Fri. THE gray-ey'd morn fmiles on the frowning
night,
Check'ring the eaftern clouds with ftreaks of light.
Now ere the fun advance his burning eye,
The day to chear, and night's dank dew to dry,
I muft fill up this ofier cage of ours
With baleful weeds, and precious juiced flowers.
O mickle is the powerful grace, that lies
In plants, herbs, ftones, and their true qualities.
For nought fo vile, that on the earth doth live,
But to the earth fome fpecial good doth give :
Nor ought fo good, but ftrain'd from that fair ufe,
Revolts to vice, and ftumbles on abufe.
Virtue itfelf turns vice, being mifapplied,

B

And

And vice fometimes by actions dignified.
Within the infant rind of this fmall flower
Poifon hath refidence, and medicine power:
For this being fmelt, with that fenfe chears each part;
Being tafted, flays all fenfes with the heart.
Two fuch oppofed foes encamp them ftill
In man, as well as herbs; Grace and rude Will:
And where the worfer is predominant,
Full foon the canker death eats up that plant.

Enter Romeo.

Rom. Good-morrow, father.

Fri. Benedicite.

What early tongue fo fweet faluteth me?
Young fon, it argues a diftemper'd head,
So foon to bid good-morrow to thy pillow;
Care keeps his watch in every old man's eye,
And where care lodgeth, fleep will never bide;
But where with unftuft brain unbruifed youth
Doth couch his limbs, there golden fleep refides,
Therefore thy earlinefs affureth me
Thou art up rouz'd by fome diftemp'rature;
What is the matter, fon?

Rom. I tell thee ere thou ask it me again;
J have been feafting with mine enemy,
Where to the heart's core one hath wounded me,
That's by me wounded; both our remedies
Within thy help and holy phyfick lie.

Fri. Be plain, good fon, and homely in thy drift.

Rom. Then plainly know, my heart's dear love is fet
On *Juliet, Capulet*'s fair daughter;
As mine on hers, fo hers is fet on mine:
When, and where, and how
We met, we woo'd, and made exchange of vows,
I'll tell thee as we pafs; but this I beg
That thou confent to marry us to day.

Fri. Holy faint *Francis,* what a change is here!
But tell me, fon, and call thy reafon home,
Is not this love the offspring of thy folly,
Bred from thy wantonnefs and thoughtlefs brain?
Be heedful, youth, and fee you ftop betimes,
Left that thy rafh ungovernable paffions,
O'er-leaping duty, and each due regard,

Hurry

Hurry thee on, thro' short-liv'd, dear-bought pleasures,
To cureless woes, and lasting Penitence.

Rom. I pray thee, chide me not, she whom I love,
Doth give me grace for grace, and love for love:
Do thou with heav'n smile upon our union ;
Do not withhold thy benediction from us,
But make two hearts, by holy marriage one.

Fri. Well, come, my pupil, go along with me.
In one respect I'll give thee my assistance ;
For this alliance may so happy prove,
To turn your houshold rancour to pure love.

Rom. O let us hence, Love stands on sudden haste.

Fri. Wisely and slow ; they stumble that run fast.

[*Exeunt.*

SCENE IV.

The STREET.

Enter Benvolio *and* Mercutio.

Mer. WHERE the devil should this *Romeo* be ?
came he not home to night ?

Ben. Not to his father's ; I spoke with his man.

Mer. Why that same pale hard-hearted wench, that
Rosaline, torments him so, that he will sure run mad.

Ben. *Tibalt,* the kinsman to old *Capulet,* hath sent
a letter to his father's house.

Mer. A challenge, on my life.

Ben. *Romeo* will answer it.

Mer. Alas, poor *Romeo,* he is already dead ! stabb'd
with a white wench's black eye, run through the ear
with a love-song, the very pin of his heart cleft with the
blind bow-boy's but-shaft ; and is he a man to encounter
Tibalt ?

Ben. Why, what is *Tibalt ?*

Mer. Oh he's the courageous captain of compliments ;
he fights as you sing prick-song, keeps time, distance, and
proportion ; rests his minum, one, two, and the third in
your bosom ; the very butcher of a silk button, a duellist,
a duellist ; a gentleman of the very first house, of the

B 2   first

firſt and ſecond cauſe; ah the immortal paſſado, the punto reverſo, the hay——

Ben. The what?

Mer. The pox of ſuch antick liſping affected phantaſies, theſe new tuners of accents:——Jeſu, a very good blade,——a very tall man——a very good whore.——Why, is not this a lamentable thing, grandſire, that we ſhould be thus afflicted with theſe ſtrange flies, theſe faſhion-mongers, theſe *pardonnez-moy's?*

Ben. Here comes *Romeo.*

Mer. Without his roe, like a dried herring. O fleſh, fleſh, how art thou fiſhified? Now is he for the numbers that *Petarch* flowed in: *Laura* to his lady was but a kitchen-wench; marry ſhe had a better love to berime her: *Dido* a dowdy, *Cleopatra* a gipſie, *Helen* and *Hero* hildings and harlots: *Thisbe* a gray eye or ſo, but not to the purpoſe.

Enter Romeo.

Signior *Romeo, bonjour,* there's a *French* ſalutation for you.

Rom. Good morrow to you both.

Mer. You gave us the counterfeit fairly laſt night.

Rom. What counterfeit did I give you?

Mer. The ſlip, Sir, the ſlip: can you not conceive?

Rom. Pardon, *Mercutio,* my buſineſs was great, and in ſuch a caſe as mine, a man may ſtrain curteſy.

Enter Nurſe and her Man.

Rom. A ſayle! a ſayle.

Mer. Two, two, a ſhirt and a ſmock.

Nurſe. Peter.

Pet. Anon,

Nurſe. My fan, *Peter.*

Mer. Do, good *Peter,* to hide her face.

Nurſe. God ye good-morrow, gentlemen.

Mer. God ye good den, fair gentlewoman.

Nurſe. Gentlemen, can any of you tell me where I may find young *Romeo?*

Rom. I am the youngeſt of that name, for fault of a worſe.

Nurſe. You ſay well.

If you be he, ſir,

I deſire ſome *confidence* with you.

Ben. She will *indite* him to ſupper preſently.

Mer.

Mer. A bawd, a bawd, a bawd: So ho.

Rom. What haft thou found?

Mar. No hare, Sir, but a bawd. *Romeo,* will you come to your father's? we'll to dinner thither.

Rom. I will follow you.

Mar. Farewel, ancient lady.

[*Exeunt* Mercutio, Benvolio.

Nurfe. I pray you, Sir, what faucy merchant was this that was fo full of his roguery?

Rom. A gentleman, nurfe, that loves to hear himfelf talk, and will fpeak more in a minute, than he will ftand to in a month.

Nurfe. An' a fpeak any thing againft me, I'll take him down an' he were luftier than he is, and twenty fuch jacks: and if I cannot, I'll find thofe that fhall. Scurvy knave, I am none of his flirt-gills; and thou muft ftand by too, and fuffer every knave to ufe me at his pleafure.

[*To her man.*

Pet. I faw no man ufe you at his pleafure: if I had, my weapon fhould quickly have been out, I warrant you. I dare draw as foon as another man, if I fee occafion in a good quarrel, and the law on my fide.

Nurfe. Now, afore God, I am fo vext, that every part about me quivers——Scurvy knave! Pray you, Sir, a word: and as I told you, my young lady bid me enquire you out. What fhe bid me fay, I will keep to myfelf: but firft let me tell ye, if ye fhould lead her into fool's paradife, as they fay, it were a very grofs kind of behaviour, as they fay; for the gentlewoman is young, and therefore if you fhould deal double with her, truly it were an ill thing to be offered to any gentlewoman.

Rom. Commend me to thy lady and miftrefs, I proteft unto thee——

Nurfe. Good heart, and i'faith I will tell her as much; Lord, lord, fhe will be a joyful woman.

Rom. What wilt thou tell her, nurfe? thou doft not mark me.

Nurfe. I will tell her, Sir, that you do proteft; which, as I take it, is a gentleman-like offer.

Rom. Bid her devife fome means to come to fhrift this afternoon.

And

And there she shall at friar *Lawrence*'s cell
Be shriv'd and married ; here's for thy pains.

   Nurse No truly, Sir, not a penny.

   Rom. Go to, I say, you shall.

   Nurse. This afternoon, Sir ? well, she shall be there.

   Rom. And stay, good nurse, behind the abbey-wall :
Within this hour my man shall be with thee,
And bring thee cords made like a tackled stair,
Which to the high top gallant of my joy
Must be my convoy in the secret night.
Farewel, be trusty, and I'll quit thy pains.

   Nurse. Well, Sir, my mistress is the sweetest lady ;
lord, lord, when t'was a little prating thing————O,
there is a noble man in town, one *Paris*, that would fain
lay knife aboard ; but she, good soul, had as lieve see a
toad, a very toad, as see him : I anger her sometimes,
and tell her that *Paris* is the properer man ; but I'll warrant you, when I say so, she looks as pale as any clout in
the versal world. Commend me to my lady——

   Rom. Commend me to my lady——   [*Exit* Romeo.

   Nurse. A thousand times. *Peter ?*

   Pet. Anon.

   Nurse. Take my fan, and go before.   [*Exeunt.*

SCENE V.

Capulet's *House.*

Enter Juliet.

   Jul. THE clock struck nine, when I did send the
nurse :
In half an hour she promis'd to return.
Perchance she cannot meet him—That's not so—
Oh she is lame : love's heralds should be thoughts,
Which ten times faster glide than the sun-beams,
Driving back shadows over lowring hills.
Therefore do nimble-pinion'd doves draw love,
And therefore hath the wind-swift *Cupid* wings.
Now is the sun upon the highmost hill
Of this day's journey, and from nine till twelve—
are is three long hours—and yet she is not come ;
Had she affections, and warm youthful blood,

                        She'd

She'd be as fwift in motion as a ball,
My words would bandy her to my fweet love,
And his to me.

Enter Nurfe.

O Heav'n! fhe comes. What news?
Haft thou met with him? fend thy man away.

Nurfe. Peter, ftay at the gate.　　　　[*Exit* Peter.

Jul. How now, fweet Nurfe:
O Lord, why look'ft thou fad?

Nurfe. I am a weary, let me reft a while;
Fy, how my bones ake, what a jaunt have I had?

Jul. Nay, come, I pray thee fpeak—Good nurfe, fpeak.
Is thy news good or bad? anfwer to that.
Say either, and I'll ftay the circumftance:
Let me be fatisfied, is't good or bad?

Nurfe. Well, you have made a fimple choice; you
know not how to choofe a man: Go thy ways, wench,
ferve God —— What, have you dined at home?

Jul. No, no,——but all this did I know before:
What fays he of our marriage? what of that?

Nurfe. Lord, how my head akes? what a head have I?
It beats as it would fall in twenty pieces.
My back o't'other fide——O my back, my back:
Befhrew your heart, for fending me about,
To catch my death with jaunting up and down.

Jul. I'faith I'm forry that thou art fo ill.
Sweet, fweet, fweet nurfe, tell me, what fays my love?

Nurfe. Your love fays like an honeft gentleman,
And a courteous, and a kind, and a handfome,
And I warrant a virtuous——where is your mother?

Jul. Where is my mother? why fhe is within,
Where fhould fhe be? how odly thou reply'ft!
Your love fays like an honeft gentleman:
Where is your mother——

Nurfe. O our lady dear,
Are you fo hot? marry come up! I trow.
Is this the pultice for my aking bones?
Hence-forward do your meffages yourfelf.

Jul. Here's fuch a coil; come, what fays *Romeo?*
Nurfe. Have you got leave to go to fhrift to-day?
Jul. I have.

Nurse. Then hie you hence to friar *Lawrence'* cell,
There ſtays a husband to make you a wife.
Now comes the wanton blood up in your cheeks————
Hie you to church, I muſt another way,
To fetch a ladder, by the which your love
Muſt climb a bird's neſt ſoon, when it is dark.
I am the drudge and toil in your delight,
But you ſhall bear the burden ſoon at night.
Go. I'll to dinner, hie you to the cell.
    Jul. Hie to high fortune:
Honeſt nurſe, farewel.   [*Exeunt.*

S C E N E   VI.

The Monaſtery.

Enter Friar Lawrence *and* Romeo.

Fri. SO ſmile the heav'ns upon this holy act,
    That after-hours of ſorrow chide us not!
    Rom. Amen, amen, but come what ſorrow can,
It cannot countervail th' exchange of joy,
That one ſhort minute gives me in her ſight:
Do thou but cloſe our hands with holy words,
Then love-devouring death do what he dare,
It is enough I may but call her mine.
    Fri. Theſe violent delights have violent ends,
And in their triumph die like fire and powder,
Which as they meet, conſume. The ſweeteſt honey
Is loathſome in its own deliciouſneſs,
And in the taſte confounds the appetite:
Therefore love mod'rately.

Enter Juliet.

Here comes the lady.   O ſo light a foot
Will ne'er wear out the everlaſting flint;
A lover may beſtride the goſſamour,
That idles in the wanton ſummer air,
And yet not fall, ſo light is vanity.
    Jul. Good-even to my ghoſtly confeſſor.
    Fri. Romeo ſhall thank thee, daughter, for us both.
    Rom. Ah *Juliet*, if the meaſure of thy joy

                                                    Be

Be heapt like mine, and that thy skill be more
To blazon it; then sweeten with thy breath
This neighbour air, and let rich musick's tongue
Unfold th' imagin'd happiness, that both
Receive in either, by this dear encounter.

Jul. Conceit more rich in matter than in words,
Brags of his substance, not of ornament:
They are but beggars that can count their worth;
But my true love is grown to such excess,
I cannot sum up one half of my wealth.

Fri. Come, come with me;
For, by your leaves, you shall not stay alone,
Till holy church incorp'rate two in one.   [*Exeunt.*

ACT III. SCENE I.

The STREET.

Enter Mercutio, Benvolio, *and servants.*

BENVOLIO.

I Pray thee, good *Mercutio*, let's retire,
  The day is hot, the *Capulets* abroad,
  And if we meet we shall not 'scape a brawl.

Mer. Thou art like one of those fellows, that when he
enters the confines of a tavern, claps me his sword upon
the table, and says, God send me no need of thee; and
by the operation of a second cup, draws it on the drawer,
when indeed there is no need.

Ben. Am I like such a fellow?

Mer. Come, come, thou art as hot a *Jack* in thy
mood as any in *Italy*; an' there were two such, we should
have none shortly, for one would kill the other. Thou!
why thou wilt quarrel with a man that hath a hair more,
or a hair less in his beard than thou hast: thou wilt
quarrel with a man for cracking nuts, having no other
reason, but because thou hast hazel eyes; thou hast

B 5   quarrell'd

quarrell'd with a man for coughing in the ſtreet, becauſe
he hath wakened thy dog that hath lain aſleep in the ſun.
Didſt thou not fall out with a tailor for wearing his new
doublet before *Eaſter* ? with another, for tying his new
ſhoes with old ribband ? and yet thou wilt tutor me for
quarrelling !

Ben. If I were ſo apt to quarrel as thou art, any man
ſhould buy the fee ſimple of my life for an hour and a
quarter.

Enter Tibalt, Petruchio, *and others.*

Ben. By my head, here come the *Capulets.*

Mer. By my heel, I care not.

Tib. Be near at hand, for I will ſpeak to them :
Gentlemen, good den, a word with one of you.

Mer. And but one word with one of us ? couple it with
ſomething, make it a word and a blow.

Tib. You ſhall find me apt enough to that, Sir, if you
will give me occaſion.

Mer. Could you not take ſome occaſion without giving ?

Tib. Mercutio, thou conſort'ſt with *Romeo.*

Mer. Conſort ? what, doſt thou make us minſtrels ! if
thou make minſtrels of us, look to hear nothing but diſ-
cords : here' my fiddleſtick, here's that ſhall make you
dance, zounds ! conſort !

[*Laying his hand on his Sword.*

Ben. We talk here in the publick haunt of men :
Either withdraw into ſome private place,
Or reaſon coldly of your grievances,
Or elſe depart ; here all eyes gaze on us.

Mer. Mens eyes were made to look, and let them
gaze,
I will not budge for no man's pleaſure, I.

Enter Romeo.

Tib. Well, peace be with you, Sir, here comes my
man.

Mer. But I'll be hang'd, Sir, if he wear your livery.

Tib. Romeo, the love I bear thee can afford
No better term than this ; thou art a villain.

Rom. Tibalt, the reaſon that I have to love thee,
Doth much excuſe the appertaining rage

To

To fuch a greeting: villain I am none,
Therefore farewel, I fee thou know'ft me not.

Tib. Boy, this fhall not excufe the injuries
That thou haft done me, therefore turn and draw.

Rom. I do proteft I never injur'd thee,
But love thee better than thou canft devife;
And fo, good *Capulet* (whofe name I tender
As dearly as my own) be fatisfied.

Mer. O calm, difhonourable vile fubmiffion!
Ha! *la ftoccata* carries it away——*Tibalt*——you rat-
catcher.

Tib. What would'ft thou have with me?

Mer. Will you pluck your fword out of his pilcher by
the ears? Make hafte, left mine be about your ears ere
it be out.

Tib. I am for you, Sir.   [*Drawing.*

Rom. Gentle *Mercutio.* put thy raper up.

Mer. Come, Sir, your paffado. [*Mer. and Tib. fight.*

Rom. Draw, *Benvolio*—beat down their weapons——
Gentlemen—for fhame forbear this outrage——
Hold *Tibalt*, good *Mercutio* —— [*Exit* Tibalt.

Mer. I am hurt——
A plague of both your houfes! I am fped:
Is he gone, and hath nothing?

Rom. What, art thou hurt?

Mer. Ay, ay, a fcratch, a fcratch; marry 'tis enough:
Go, fetch a furgeon.

Rom. Courage, man, the hurt cannot be much;

Mer. No, 'tis not fo deep as a well, nor fo wide as a
church-door, but 'tis enough, 'twill ferve: I am pepper'd,
I warrant, for this world: a plague of both your houfes!
What? a braggart, a rogue, a villain, that fights by the
book of arithmetick? why the devil came you between
us? I was hurt under your arm.

Rom. I thought all for the beft.

Mer. Help me into fome houfe, *Benvolio,*
Or I fhall faint; a plague o' both your houfes!
They have made worms meat of me,
I have it, and foundly too; plague take your houfes;
Your *Mountagues* and *Capulets* together! [*Exe.* Mer. Ben.

S C E N E

S C E N E II.

Rom. THIS gentleman, the prince's near allie,
My very friend, hath got his mortal hurt
In my behalf; my reputation's stain'd
With *Tibalt*'s slander : O sweet *Juliet*,
Thy beauty's power makes me effeminate,
And in my temper softned valour's steel.

Enter Benvolio.

Ben. O *Romeo*, *Romeo*, brave *Mercutio*'s dead,
That gallant spirit hath aspir'd the clouds,
Which too untimely here did scorn the earth.

Enter Tibalt.

Ben. Here comes the furious *Tibalt* back again.
Rom. Alive ? in triumph ? and *Mercutio* slain ?
Away to heaven respective lenity,
And fire-ey'd fury be my conduct now !
Now, *Tibalt*, take the villain back again,
That late thou gav'st me ; for *Mercutio*'s soul
Is but a little way above our heads,
And thou or I, must keep him company.

Tib. Thou wretched boy, that didst consort him here,
Shalt with him hence.

Rom. This shall determine that.

[*They fight,* Tibalt *falls.*

Ben. Romeo, away, begone :
The citizens are up, and *Tibalt* slain——
Stand not amaz'd, the prince will doom thee dead,
If thou art taken : hence, be gone, away.

Rom. O! I am fortune's fool.   [*Exit* Romeo.

S C E N E III.

Enter Prince, Mountague, Capulet, *Citizens, &c.*

Prince. WHERE are the vile beginners of this
fray ?
Be . O noble prince, I can discover all.

The

The unlucky manage of this fatal quarrel:
There lies the man flain by young *Romeo*,
That flew thy kinfman brave *Mercutio*.

Cap. Unhappy fight! alas the blood is fpill'd
Of my dear kinfman———Now as thou art a Prince,
For blood of ours, fhed blood of *Mountague*.

Prince. Benvolio, who began this fray?

Ben. Tibalt here flain;
Romeo befpake him fair, bid him bethink
How nice the quarrel was, and urg'd withal
Your high difpleafure: all this uttered
With gentle breath, calm look, knees humbly bow'd,
Could not make truce with the unruly fpleen
Of *Tibalt*, deaf to peace, but he that tilts
With piercing fteel at bold *Mercutio*'s breaft;
Who all as hot, turns deadly point to point,
And with a martial fcorn, with one hand beats
Cold death afide, and with the other fends
It back to *Tibalt*, whofe dexterity
Retorts it: *Romeo*, he cries aloud
Hold friends, friends part! and fwifter than his tongue,
His agil arm beats down their fatal points,
And 'twixt them rufhes; underneath whofe arm
An envious thruft from *Tibalt* hit the life
Of ftout *Mercutio*, and then *Tibalt* fled;
But and by comes back to *Romeo*,
Who had but newly entertain'd revenge,
And to't they go like light'ning: for ere I
Could draw to part them, was ftout *Tibalt* flain,
And as he fell, did *Romeo* turn to fly:
This is the Truth, or let *Benvolio* fuffer.

Cap. He is a kinfman to the *Mountague*,
Affection makes him falfe;
I beg for juftice; juftice, gracious Prince;
Romeo flew *Tibalt*, *Romeo* muft not live.

Prin. Romeo flew him, he flew *Mercutio*;
And now the price of his dear blood hath pay'd.

Mount. Romeo but took the forfeit life of *Tibalt*.

Prin. And we for that offence do banifh him.
I have an int'reft in your heady brawls,
My blood doth flow from brave *Mercutio*'s wounds.

But

But I'll amerce you with so strong a fine,
That you shall all repent my loss in him.
I will be deaf to pleading and excuse,
Nor tears nor prayers shall purchase our repeal:
Therefore use none; let *Romeo* be gone,
Else when he is found, that hour is his last.
Bear hence this body, and attend our will:
Mercy but murders, pardoning those that kill. [*Exeunt.*

SCENE IV.

An Apartment in Capulet's *House.*

Enter Juliet alone.

Jul. GALLOP apace, you fiery-footed steeds,
To *Phœbus'* mansion; such a waggoner
As *Phaeton,* would whip you to the west,
And bring in cloudy night immediately.
Spread thy close curtain, love-performing night,
That th' run-away s eyes may wink; and *Romeo*
Leap to these arms, untalkt of and unseen.
Come night, come *Romeo!* come thou day in night!
For thou wilt lye upon the wings of night,
Whiter than snow upon the raven's back:
Give me my *Romeo,* night, and when he dies
Take him and cut him out in little stars,
And he will make the face of heav'n so fine,
That all the world will be in love with night,
And pay no worship to the garish sun: ———
O, I have bought the mansion of a love,
But not possess'd it; so tedious is this day,
As is the night before some festival,
To an impatient child that hath new robes,
And may not wear them. O here comes my nurse!

Enter Nurse.

And she brings news, and every tongue that speaks
But *Romeo's* name, speaks heav'nly eloquence;
Now nurse, what news?
Why dost thou wring thy hands?

Nurse. Ah welladay he's dead, he's dead, he's dead!
We are undone, lady, we are undone————

Jul. Can heav'n be so envious?

Nurse. Romeo can,
Though heav'n cannot. O *Romeo! Romeo!*

Jul. What devil art thou, that does torment me thus?
This torture should be roar'd in difmal hell.
Hath *Romeo* slain himself? say thou but ay,
And that bare little word shall poison more
Than the earth darting eye of cockatrice.

Nurse. I saw the wound, I saw it with mine eyes,
Here on his manly breast.
A piteous coarse, a bloody piteous coarse;
I swooned at the sight.

Jul. O break my heart—poor bankrupt, break at once!
To prison, eyes! ne'er look on liberty;
Vile earth to earth refign, end motion here,
And thou and *Romeo* prefs one heavy bier!

Nurse. O *Tibalt, Tibalt,* the beft friend I had;
That ever I should live to fee thee dead.

Jul. What storm is this that blows so contrary?
Is *Romeo* flaughter'd? and is *Tibalt* dead?

Nurse. *Tibalt* is dead, and *Romeo* banished,
Romeo that kill'd him, he is banished.

Jul. O heaven! did *Romeo's* hand shed *Tibalt's* blood?

Nurse. It did, it did, alas the day! it did.

Jul. O nature! what hadst thou to do in hell,
When thou didst bower the spirit of a fiend
In mortal paradise of such sweet flesh? O that deceit
should dwell
In such a gorgeous palace.

Nurse. No faith, no honefty in men;
Shame come to *Romeo!*

Jul. Blifter'd be thy tongue,
For such a wish, he was not born to shame,
Upon his brow shame is asham'd to fit:
For 'tis a throne where honour may be crown'd,
Sole monarch of the universal earth.
O what a wretch was I to chide him so?

Nurse. Will you speak well of him that kill'd your coufin?

Jul. Shall I speak ill of him that is my husband?
Ah poor my lord, what tongue shall smooth thy name,

When

When I thy three hours wife have mangled it ?
Back, foolish tears, back to your native spring ;
Your tributary drops belong to woe,
Which you mistaking offer up to joy.
My husband lives that *Tibalt* would have slain,
And *Tibalt*'s dead that would have kill'd my husband ;
All this is comfort ; wherefore weep I then ?
Some word there was worser than *Tibalt*'s death
That murder'd me ; I would forget it fain,
But oh it presses to my memory,
Like damned guilty deeds to sinners minds ;
Tibalt is dead, and Romeo *banished,*
That *banished,* that one word *banished,*
Hath slain ten thousand *Tibalts :* In that word ·
Is father, mother, *Tibalt,* Romeo, *Juliet,*
All slain, all dead !——*Romeo is banished !*
Where is my father, and my mother, nurse ?
   Nurse. Weeping and wailing over *Tibalt*'s coarse :
Will you go to them ? I will bring you thither.
   Jul. Wash they his wounds with tears ? My eyes
               shall flow
When theirs are dry, for *Romeo*'s banishment.
   Nurse. Hie to your chamber, I'll find *Romeo,*
To comfort you. I wot well where he is.
Hark ye, your *Romeo* will be here at night ;.
I'll to him, he is hid at *Lawrence*' cell.
   Jul. O find him, give this ring to my true lord,
And bid him come to take his last farewel.   *[Exeunt.*

S C E N E V.

The Monastery.

Enter Friar Lawrence *and* Romeo.

Fri. **R**OMEO come forth, come forth thou fearful
           man,
Affliction is enamour'd of thy parts ;
And thou art wedded to calamity.
   Rom. Father, what news ? what is the prince's doom?
What sorrow craves acquaintance at my hand,
That I yet know not ?   *Fri.*

Fri. Too familiar
Is my dear fon with fuch four company,
I bring thee tidings of the prince's doom.

Rom. What lefs than death can be the prince's doom?

Fri. A gentler judgment vanifh'd from his lips,
Not body's death, but body's banifhment.

Rom. Ha! banifhment! be merciful, fay death;
For exile hath more terror in his look,
Much more than death: Do not fay banifhment;
'Tis death mif term'd calling death banifhment;
Thou cut'ft my head off with a golden ax,
And fmil'ft upon the ftroke that murders me.

Fri. O deadly fin! O rude unthankfulnefs!
Thy fault our law calls death, but the kind prince
Taking thy part hath pufh'd afide the law,
And turn'd that black word death to banifhment,
This is meer mercy, and thou feeft it not.

Rom. 'Tis torture, and not mercy: heav'n is here
Where *Juliet* lives. There's more felicity
In carrion-flies, than *Romeo:* they may feize
On the white wonder of dear *Juliet's* hand,
And fteal immortal bleffings from her lips;
But *Romeo* may not, he is banifhed!
O father, hadft thou no ftrong poifon mixt,
No fharp-ground knife, no prefent means of death,
But banifhment to torture me withal.

Fri. Fond mad-man, hear me fpeak.
I'll give thee armour to bear off that word,
Adverfity's fweet milk, philofophy,
To comfort thee tho' thou art banifhed.

Rom. Yet banifhed? hang up philofophy:
Unlefs philofophy can make a *Juliet,*
It helps not, it prevails not, talk no more——

Fri. Let me difpute with thee of thy eftate.

Rom. Thou canft not fpeak of what thou doft not feel:
Wert thou as young as I, *Juliet* thy love,
An hour but married, *Tibalt* murthered:
Doting like me, and like me banifhed;
Then might'ft thou fpeak, then might'ft thou tear thy hair,
And fall upon the ground as I do now,
Taking the meafure of an unmade grave.

[Throwing himfelf on the ground.

Fri. Arife, one knocks; good *Romeo,* hide thyfelf.

[Knock within.

Rom. Not I, unleſs the breath of heart-ſick groans,
Miſt-like, infold me from the ſearch of eyes.

Fri. Hark how they knock——*Romeo*, ariſe.
Who's there?
Thou wilt be taken—ſtay a while—ſtand up; [*Knocks.*
Run to my ſtudy—— By and by——God's will;
What wilfulneſs is this!—I come, I come. [*Knock.*
Who knocks ſo hard? whence come you? what's your will?

Nurſe [*within.*] Let me come in, and you ſhall know
my errand:
I come from lady *Juliet.*

Fri. Welcome then.

Enter Nurſe.

Nurſe. O holy Friar, oh tell me, holy Friar,
Where is my lady's lord? where's *Romeo?*

Fri. There, on the ground, with his own tears made
drunk.

Nurſe. O he is even in my miſtreſs's caſe,
Juſt in her caſe: O *Juliet, Juliet!*

Rom. Speak'ſt thou of *Juliet?* how is it with her?
Since I have ſtain'd the childhood of our joy
With blood,
Where is ſhe? how does ſhe? what ſays ſhe?

Nurſe. O ſhe ſays nothing, Sir, but weeps and weeps,
And now falls on her bed, and then ſtarts up,
And *Tibalt* cries, and then on *Romeo* calls,
And then down falls again.

Rom. As if that name
Shot from the deadly level of a gun
Did murder her. Tell me, Friar, tell me,
In what vile part of this anatomy
Doth my name lodge? tell me, that I may ſack
The hateful manſion.

Fri. Hold thy deſperate hand:
Art thou a man? thy form cries out, thou art;
Thy tears are womaniſh, thy wild acts note
Th' unreaſonable fury of a beaſt.
Thou haſt amaz'd me. By my holy order,
I thought thy diſpoſition better-temper'd.
Haſt thou ſlain *Tibalt?* wilt thou ſlay thyſelf?
And ſlay thy lady too, that lives in thee?
What, rouſe thee, man, thy *Juliet* is alive,   Go

Go get thee to thy love, as was decreed;
Afcend her chamber, hence and comfort her:
But look thou ftay not 'till the watch be fet,
For then thou can'ft not pafs to *Mantua*,
Where thou fhalt live, 'till we can find a time
To blaze your marriage, reconcile your friends,
Beg pardon of thy prince, and call thee back
With twenty hundred thoufand times more joy,
Than thou went'ft forth in lamentation.
Go before, nurfe; commend me to thy lady,
And bid her haften all the houfe to reft,
Romeo is coming.

    Nurfe. O lord, I could have ftaid here all night long
To hear good counfel: oh, what learning is!
My lord, I'll tell my lady you will come.

    Rom. Do fo, and bid my fweet prepare to chide.

    Nurfe. Here, Sir, a ring fhe bid me give you, Sir:
Hie you, make hafte, for it grows very late.

    Rom. How well my comfort is reviv'd by this!

    Fri. Sojourn in *Mantua*; I'll find out your man,
And he fhall fignify from time to time
Every good hap to you that chances here:
Give me thy hand, 'tis late, farewel, good night.

    Rom. But that a joy, paft joy, calls out on me,
It were a grief, fo foon to part with thee.   [*Exeunt.*

S C E N E VI.
Capulet's *Houfe.*
Enter Capulet, *Lady* Capulet, *and* Paris.

Cap. THings have fall'n out, Sir, fo unluckily,
        That we have had no time to move our
                    daughter:
Look you, fhe lov'd her kinfman *Tibalt* dearly,
And fo did I —— Well, we were born to die ——
'Tis very late, fhe'll not come down to night.

    Par. Thefe times of grief afford no time to woo:
Madam, good night, commend me to your daughter.

    Cap. Sir *Paris*, I will make a defperate tender
Of my child's love: I think fhe will be rul'd
In all refpects by me, nay more, I doubt it not.
But foft; what day? Well, *Wednefday* is too foon,

                               On

On *Thursday* (let it be) you shall be marry'd.
We'll keep no great ado —— a friend or two——
For, hark you, *Tibalt* being slain so late,
It may be thought we held him carelesly,
Being our kinsman, if we revel much :
Therefore we'll have some half a dozen friends,
And there's an end.   But what say you to *Thursday* ?

   Par. My lord, I would that *Thursday* were to-morrow.

   Cap. Well, get you gone —— on *Thursday* be it then:
Go you to *Juliet* ere you go to bed ;   [*To Lady* Cap.
Prepare her, wife, against this wedding-day.
Farewel, my lord — light to my chamber, hoa !
Good-night.   [*Exeunt.*

S C E N E   VII.

The Garden.

***Enter* Romeo *and* Juliet *above at a window ; a ladder of*
Ropes set.

Jul. WILT thou be gone? it is not yet near day :
      It was the Nightingale, and not the Lark,
That pierc'd the fearful hollow of thine ear ;
Nightly she sings on yon pomgranate tree :
Believe me, love, it was the nightingale.

   Rom. It was the Lark, the herald of the morn,
No Nightingale.   Look, love, what envious streaks
Do lace the severing clouds in yonder east :
Night's candles are burnt out, and jocund day
Stands tiptoe on the misty mountain tops,
I must be gone and live, or stay and die.

   Jul. Yon light is not day-light, I know it well ;
It is some meteor that the sun exhales,
To be this night a torch-bearer,
And light thee on thy way to *Mantua ;*
Then stay a while, thou shalt not go so soon.

   Rom. Let me be ta'en ; let me be put to death,
If thou wilt have it so, I am content.
I'll say yon gray is not the morning eye,
'Tis but the pale reflex of *Cynthia's* brow,
I'll say, tis not the Lark whose notes do beat,
The vaulty heav'ns so high above our heads;

                              Come

Come death and welcome : *Juliet* wills it so.
What says my love ? let's talk, it is not day.

Jul. It is, it is, hie hence away, be gone ;
It is the Lark that sings so out of tune,
Straining harsh discords, and unpleasing sharps.
O now be gone, more light and light it grows.

Rom. More light and light ? —more dark and dark our
Farewel, my love : one kiss, and I'll be gone. [woes.

Enter Nurse.

Nurse. Madam.
Jul. Nurse
Nurse. Your lady mother's coming to your chamber :
The day is broke, be wary, look about.

Jul. Art thou gone so ? love ! lord ! ah husband, friend !
I must hear from thee ev'ry day in th' hour,
For in love's hours there are many days.
O by this count I shall be much in years,
Ere I again behold my *Romeo.*

Rom. Farewel I will omit no opportunity,
That may convey my greetings to my love.

Jul. O think'st thou we shall ever meet again ?

Rom. I doubt it not, and all these woes shall serve
For sweet discourses, in our time to come.

Jul. O heav'n ! I have an ill-divining soul,
Methinks I see thee, now thou'rt parting from me,
As one dead in the bottom of a tomb !
Either my eye-sight fails, or thou look'st pale.

Rom. And trust me, love, in mine eye so do you:
Dry sorrow drinks our blood. Adieu !
My life, my love, my soul, Adieu ! [*Exeunt.*

S C E N E VIII.

Juliet's *Chamber.*

Enter Juliet.

Jul. OH fortune, fortune, all men call thee fickle:
If thou art fickle, what dost thou with him
That is renown'd for faith ? be fickle, fortune :

For

For then I hope thou wilt not keep him long,
But send him back again.

Enter lady Capulet.

La. Cap. Ho daughter, are you up?

Jul. Who is't that calls? is it my lady mother?
What unaccustom'd cause procures her hither?

La. Cap. Why how now, *Juliet*.

Jul. Madam, I'm not well.

La. Cap. Evermore weeping for your cousin's death?
What, wilt thou wash him from his grave with tears?

Jul. Yet let me weep for such a loss as mine.

La. Cap. I come to bring thee joyful tidings, girl.

Jul. And joy comes well in such a needful time.
What are they, I beseech your ladyship?

La. Cap. Well, well, thou hast a careful father, child;
One, who to put thee from thy heaviness,
Hath sorted out a sudden day of joy,
That thou expect'st not, nor I look'd not for.

Jul. Madam, in happy time, what day is this?

La. Cap. Marry, my child, early next *Thursday* morn,
The gallant, young and noble gentleman,
The county *Paris*, at St. *Peter*'s church,
Shall happily make thee a joyful bride.

Jul. I wonder at this haste, that I must wed
Ere he that must be husband comes to woo.
I pray you tell my lord and father, madam,
I cannot marry yet.

La Cap. Here comes your father, tell him so yourself,
And see how he will take it at your hands.

Enter Capulet *and Nurse.*

Cap. How now? a conduit, girl? what still in tears,
Evermore showering? Why how now, wife?
Have you deliver'd to her our decree?

La Cap. Ay, Sir, but she will none, she gives you thanks:
I would the fool were married to her grave.

Cap. Soft, take me with you, take me with you, wife,
How, will she none? doth she not give us thanks?
Is she not proud; doth she not count her blest,
(Unworthy as she is,) that we have wrought
So worthy gentleman to be her bridegroom?

Jul. Proud can I never be of what I hate,
But thankful even for hate, that is meant love.

Cap.

Cap. Thank me no thankings,
But settle your fine joints againſt *Thurſday* next,
To go with *Paris* to ſaint *Peter*'s church :
Or I will drag thee on a hurdle thither.

La. Cap. Fy, fy, what, are you mad ?

Jul. Good father, I beſeech you on my knees,
Hear me with patience, but to ſpeak a word.

Cap. Hang thee, young baggage, diſobedient wretch,
I tell thee what ; get thee to church a *Thurſday*,
Or never after look me in the face.
Speak not, reply not, do not anſwer me.
Wife, we ſcarce thought us bleſt,
That God had ſent us but this only child,
But now I ſee this one is one too much,
And that we have a curſe in having her :
Out on her, hilding.

Nurſe. Heaven bleſs her :
You are to blame, my lord, to rate her ſo.

Cap. And why, my lady wiſdom ? hold your tongue,
Good prudence, ſmatter with your goſſips, go.

Nurſe. I ſpeak no treaſon.

Cap. Peace, you mumbling fool ;
Utter your gravity o'er a goſſip's bowl,
For here we need it not.

La. Cap. You are too hot.

Cap. Good wife, it makes me mad ; day, night, late,
     early,
At home, abroad ; alone, in company,
Waking or ſleeping ; ſtill my care hath been
To have her match'd ; and having now provided
A gentleman of noble parentage,
Of fair demeans ; youthful, and nobly allied,
Proportion'd as ones thought would wiſh a man :
And then to have a wretched puling fool,
A whining mammet, in her fortune's tender
To anſwer, I'll not wed, I cannot love,
I am too young, I pray you pardon me.——
But, if you will not wed, look to't, think on't,
I do not uſe to jeſt. —— *Thurſday* is near.
If you be mine, I'll give you to my friend :

If

If you be not, hang, beg, ſtarve, die i'th' ſtreets;
For by my ſoul, I'll ne'er acknowledge thee. [*Exit.*

Jul. Is there no pity ſitting in the clouds,
That ſees into the bottom of my grief?
O ſweet my mother, caſt me not away,
Delay this marriage for a month, a week,
Or if you do not, make the bridal bed
In that dim monument where *Tibalt* lies.

La. Cap. Talk not to me, for I'll not ſpeak a word:
Do as thou wilt, for I have done with thee. [*Exit.*

Jul. O heav'n! O nurſe, how ſhall this be prevented?
Alack, alack, that heav'n ſhould practiſe ſtratagems
Upon ſo ſoft a ſubject as myſelf.

Nurſe. Riſe, faith here it is:
Romeo is baniſh'd; all the world to nothing,
That he dares ne'er come back to challenge you:
Or if he do, it needs muſt be by ſtealth:
Then, ſince the caſe ſo ſtands, I think it beſt
You married with the count.

Jul. Speakeſt thou from thy heart?

Nurſe. And from my ſoul too,
Or elſe beſhrew them both.

Jul. Amen, Amen.

Nurſe. What?

Jul. Well, thou haſt comforted me marvellous much;
Go in, and tell my lady I am gone,
Having diſpleas'd my father, to *Lawrence*' cell,
To make confeſſion, and to be abſolved.

Nurſe. Marry I will, and this is wiſely done. [*Exit.*

Jul. Ancient damnation! O moſt wicked fiend!
Is it more ſin to wiſh me thus forſworn,
Or to diſpraiſe my lord with that ſame tongue
Which ſhe hath prais'd him with above compare,
So many thouſand times? go, counſellor,
Thou and my boſom henceforth ſhall be twain;
I'll to the friar to know his remedy;
If all elſe fail, myſelf have power to die. [*Exit.*

ACT

A C T IV. S C E N E I.

The Monaſtery.

Enter Friar Lawrence *and* Paris.

F R I A R.

ON *Thurſday*, Sir! the time is very ſhort.
 Par. My father *Capulet* will have it ſo,
And I am nothing ſlow to ſlack his haſte.
 Fri. You ſay, you do not know the lady's mind:
Uneven is this courſe, I like it not.
 Par. Immoderately ſhe weeps for *Tibalt*'s death,
And therefore have I little talk'd of love,
For *Venus* ſmiles not in a houſe of tears.
Now, Sir, her father counts it dangerous
That ſhe ſhould give her ſorrow ſo much ſway;
And in his wiſdom haſtes our marriage,
To ſtop the inundation of her tears;
Now do you know the reaſon of this haſte.
 Fri. I would I knew not why it ſhould be ſlow'd,
Look, Sir, here comes the lady tow'rds my cell.

Enter Juliet.

 Par. Welcome my love, my lady, and my wife.
 Jul. That may be, Sir, when I may be a wife.
 Par. That may be, muſt be, love, on *Thurſday* next.
 Jul. What muſt be, ſhall be.
 Par. Come you to make confeſſion to this father?
 Jul. To anſwer that were to confeſs to you :
Are you at leiſure, holy father, now,
Or ſhall I come to thee at evening maſs ?
 Fri. My leiſure ſerves me, penſive daughter, now.
My lord, I muſt intreat the time alone.
 Par. Heav'n ſhield, I ſhould diſturb devotion :
Juliet, farewel.

         [*Exit* Paris.

Jul. Go, ſhut the door ; and when thou haſt done ſo,
Come, weep with me, paſt hope, paſt cure, paſt help.

Fri. O *Juliet*, I already know your grief.

Jul. Tell me not, Friar, that thou know'ſt my grief,
Unleſs thou tell me how I may prevent it.
If in thy wiſdom thou canſt give no help,
Do thou but call my reſolution wiſe,
And with this ſteel I'll help it preſently.
Heav'n join'd my heart and *Romeo*'s, thou our hands,
And ere this hand, by thee to *Romeo* ſeal'd,
Shall be the label to another deed,
Or my true heart with treacherous revolt
Give to another, this ſhall ſlay them both :
Therefore out of thy long experienc'd time,
Give me ſome preſent counſel, or behold
'Twixt my extremes and me this bloody dagger
Shall play the umpire ; ————
Speak now, be brief ; for I deſire to die,
If what thou ſpeak'ſt ſpeak not of remedy.

Fri. Hold, daughter ; I do 'ſpy a kind of hope,
Which craves as deſperate an execution,
As that is deſperate which we would prevent.
If rather than to marry County *Paris*
Thou haſt the ſtrength or will to ſlay thyſelf,
Then it is likely thou wilt undertake
A thing like death to free thee from this marriage,
And if thou dar'ſt, I'll give thee remedy.

Jul. O bid me leap, rather than marry *Paris*,
From off the battlements of yonder tower ;
Or chain me to ſome ſteepy mountain's top,
Where roaring bears and ſavage lions roam ;
Or ſhut me nightly in a charnel-houſe,
O'er-cover'd quite with dead mens rattling bones,
With reeky ſhanks, and yellow chapleſs ſkulls,
Or bid me go into a new made grave,
And hide me with a dead man in his ſhroud :
Things that to hear them nam'd, have made me trem-
    ble ;
And I will do it without fear or doubt,
To live an unſtain'd wife to my ſweet love.

Fri. Hold, *Juliet*, hie thee home, get thee to bed :
(Let not thy Nurſe lie with thee in thy chamber :)

And

And when thou art alone, take thou this vial,
And this diſtilled liquor drink thou off,
When preſently through all thy veins ſhall run
A cold and drowſie humour, which ſhall ſeize
Each vital ſpirit ; for no pulſe ſhall keep
His nat'ral progreſs, but ſurceaſe to beat.
No warmth, no breath ſhall teſtify thou liv'ſt ;
The roſes in thy lips and cheeks ſhall fade
To paly aſhes ; the eyes windows fall
Like death, when he ſhuts up the day of life ;
And in this borrow'd likeneſs of ſhrunk death
Thou ſhalt continue two and forty hours,
And then awake, as from a pleaſant ſleep.
Now when the bridegroom in the morning comes
To rouſe thee from thy bed, there art thou dead :
Then as the manner of our country is,
In thy beſt robes uncover'd on the bier,
Thou ſhalt be born to that ſame ancient vault,
Where all the kindred of the *Capulets* lie.
In the mean time, againſt thou ſhalt awake,
Shall *Romeo* by my letters know our drift,
And hither ſhall he come ; and he and I
Will watch thy waking, and that very night
Shall *Romeo* bear thee hence to *Mantua* ;
If no unconſtant toy nor womaniſh fear
Abate thy valour in the acting it.

    Jul. Give me, O give me, tell me not of fear.
[*Taking the vial.*

    Fri. Hold, get you gone, be ſtrong and proſperous
In this reſolve, I'll ſend a Friar with ſpeed
To *Mantua,* with my letters to thy lord.

    Jul. Love, give me ſtrength, and ſtrength ſhall help
      afford.
Farewel, dear father ━━━━━ [*Exeunt.*

            SCENE

S C E N E II.

Capulet's *House.*

Enter Capulet, *Lady* Capulet, *and Nurfe.*

Cap. WHAT, is my daughter gone to Friar *Law-*
          rence ?
Nurfe. Ay forfooth.
Cap. Well, he may chance to do fome good on her;
A peevifh felf-will'd harlotry it is.

Enter Juliet.

Nurfe. See where fhe comes from her confeffion.
Cap. How now, my head-ftrong? where have you
          been gadding?
Jul. Where I have learnt me to repent the fin
Of difobedient oppofition
To you and your behefts; and am enjoyn'd
By holy *Lawrence,* to fall proftrate here,
And beg your pardon; pardon I befeech you!
Henceforward I am ever rul'd by you.
Cap. Send for the County, go tell him of this,
I'll have this knot knit up to-morrow morning.
Jul. I met the youthful lord at *Lawrence*' cell,
And gave him what becoming love I might,
Not ftepping o'er the bounds of modefty.
Cap. This is as't fhould be.
Now afore heav'n this reverend holy Friar,
All our whole city is much bound to him.
Jul. Nurfe, will you go with me into my clofet,
To help me fort fuch needful ornaments
As you think fit to furnifh me to-morrow.

La Cap.

La. Cap. No not till *Thursday*, there is time enough.

Cap. Go, Nurse, go with her; we'll to church to-
morrow.   [*Exeunt* Juliet *and Nurse.*

La. Cap. We shall be short in our provision;
'Tis now near night.

Cap. Tush, all things shall be well,
Go thou to *Juliet*, help to deck up her:
I'll not to bed, but walk myself to *Paris*,
T' appoint him 'gainst to-morrow. My heart's light,
Since this same wayward girl is so reclaim'd.

                    [*Exeunt* Capulet *and lady* Capulet.

S C E N E   III.

Juliet's *Chamber.*

Enter Juliet *and* Nurse.

Jul. AY, those attires are best; but, gentle Nurse,
I pray thee leave me to myself to night:
For I have need of many orisons
To move the heav'ns to smile upon my state,
Which well thou know'st is cross and full of sin.

Enter Lady Capulet.

La. Cap. What, are you busy? do you need my help?
Jul. No, madam, we have cull'd such necessaries
As are behoveful for our state to-morrow:
So please you, let me now be left alone,
And let the Nurse this night sit up with you;
For I am sure you have your hands full all,
In this so sudden business.

La. Cap. Then good night:
Get thee to bed and rest, for thou hast need. [*Exeunt.*

Jul. Farewel,——heav'n knows when we shall meet
again!
I have a faint cold fear thrills through my veins,
That almost freezes up the heat of life.
I'll call them back again to comfort me.
Nurse,——yet what should they do here?

C 3   **My**

My difmal fcene I needs muft act alone:

[*Takes out the phial.*

Come, vial——What if this mixture do not work at all?
Shall I of force be married to the Count?
No, no, this fhall forbid it ; lie thou there ——

[*Pointing to a dagger.*

What if it be a poifon, which the Friar
Subt'ly hath miniftred, to have me dead,
Left in this marriage he fhould be difhonour'd,
Becaufe he married me before to *Romeo* ?
I fear it is ; and yet methinks it fhould not,
For he hath ftill been tried, a holy man ——
How, if when I am laid into the tomb,
I wake before the time that *Romeo*
Comes to redeem me ? there's a fearful point !
Shall I not then be ftifled in the vault,
To whofe foul mouth no healthfom air breathes in ?
Or if I live, is it not very like
The horrible conceit of death and night,
Together with the terror of the place,
(As in a vault, an ancient receptacle,
Where for thefe many hundred years, the bones
Of all my buried anceftors are pack'd ;
Where bloody *Tibalt*, yet but green in earth,
Lies feftring in his fhroud ; where, as they fay,
At fome hours in the night fpirits refort —)
Oh! if I wake, fhall I not be diftraught,
(Invironed with all thefe hideous fears,)
And madly play with my forefathers joints,
And pluck the mangled *Tibalt* from his fhroud ?
And in this rage, with fome great kinfman's bone
As with a club, dafh out my defp'rate brains ?
O look ! methinks I fee my coufin's ghoft
Seeking out *Romeo* —— Stay, *Tibalt*, ftay !
Romeo, I come ! this do I drink to thee.   [*Drinks.*

[*She throws herfelf on the bed.*

Alas, alas! is it not like, that I
So early waking, wt with loathfome smells
and shrieks like mandrakes torn out of the earth
That living mortals hearing them run mad —S C E N E

S C E N E. IV.

A HALL.

Enter Lady Capulet *and Nurse.*

La Cap. HOLD, take these keys, and fetch more
spices, Nurse.

Nurse. They call for dates and quinces in the pastry.

Enter Capulet *and Lady meeting.*

Cap. Come, stir, stir, stir, the second cock hath
crow'd,
The curphew bell hath rung, 'tis three o'clock ;
Look to the bak'd meats, good *Angelica,*
Spare not for cost.

Nurse. Go, you cot-quean go ;
Get you to bed ; faith you'll be sick to-morrow
For this night's watching.

Cap. No not a whit : what, I have watch'd ere now
All night for a less cause, and ne'er been sick.
[*Play musick,*
The County will be here with musick straight,
For so he said he would——I hear him near.
Nurse,—wife,—what ho ? what nurse, I say ?

Enter Nurse,

Go waken *Juliet,* go and trim her up.
I'll go and chat with *Paris* : hie, make haste ;
Make haste, I say.   ·[*Exit* Capulet.

C 4   SCENE

SCENE V.

SCENE *draws and discovers* Juliet *on a bed.*

Nurse. MIstress, what mistress! *Juliet*—— Fast, I
                    warrant her,
Why, lamb—why, lady—Fy, you slug-a-bed———
Why, love, I say—Madam, sweet-heart—why, bride—
What, not a word! you take your pennyworths now;
Sleep for a week; for the next night I warrant,
That you shall rest but little—God forgive me———
Marry and amen—How sound is she asleep?
I must needs wake her: Madam, madam, madam,
Ay, let the County take you in your bed——
He'll fright you up, i'faith. Will it not be?
What drest, and in your cloaths—and down again!
I must needs wake you: Lady, lady, lady,——
Alas, alas! help! help! my lady's dead,
O well-a-day, that ever I was born?
Ho! my lord, my lady!

Enter Lady Capulet.

La. Cap. What noise is here?
Nurse. O lamentable day!
La. Cap. What is the matter?
Nurse. Look——oh heavy day!
La. Cap. Oh me, my child, my only life!
Revive, look up, or I will die with thee:
Help, help! call help.

Enter Capulet.

Cap. For shame bring *Juliet* forth, her lord is come.
Nurse. She's dead, she's dead: alack the day!
Cap. Ha! let me see her———Out alas, she's cold,
Her blood is settled, and her joints are stiff,
Life and these lips have long been separated:
Death lies on her, like an untimely frost
Upon the sweetest flower of the field.
Accursed time! unfortunate old man!

                                        Enter

Enter Friar Lawrence, *and* Paris *with Musicians.*

Fri. Come, is the bride ready to go to church?

Cap. Ready to go, but never to return.
O son, the night before the wedding-day
Death has embrac'd thy wife: see, there she lies.
Flower as she was, nipp'd in the bud by him!
Oh *Juliet*, oh my Child, Child!

Par. Have I thought long to see this morning's face,
And doth it give me such a sight as this?

La. Cap. Accurst, unhappy, wretched, hateful day.

Cap. Most miserable hour, that Time e'er saw
In lasting labour of his pilgrimage.
But one, poor one, one poor and loving child,
But one thing to enjoy and solace in,
And cruel death hath catcht it from my sight.

Fri. Your daughter lives in peace and happiness;
Heav'n and yourself had part in this fair maid,
Now, heav'n hath all————
Come, stick your rosemary on this fair corps,
And as the custom of our country is,
Convey her where her ancestors lie tomb'd.

Cap. All things that we ordained to festival,
Turn from their office to black funeral:
Our instruments, to melancholy bells;
Our wedding chear, to a sad burial feast;
Our solemn hymns to sullen dirges change;
And bridal flowers serve for a buried coarse.   [*Exeunt.*

AC T

ACT V. SCENE I.

The inside of a Church.

Enter the funeral procession of *Juliet*, in which the following Dirge is sung.

CHORUS.

R*ISE, rise!*
 Heart-breaking sighs
The woe-fraught bosom swell;
 For sighs alone,
 And dismal moan,
Should echo Juliet's *knell.*

AIR.

She's gone — the sweetest flow'r of May,
 That blooming blest our sight;
Those eyes which shone like breaking day,
 Are set in endless night!

CHORUS.

Rise, rise! &c.

AIR.

She's gone, she's gone, nor leaves behind
So fair a form, so pure a mind;
How could'st thou, Death, at once destroy,
The Lover's *hope, the* Parent's *joy?*

CHORUS.

Rise, Rise! &c.

AIR.

A I R.

Thou spotless soul, look down below,
Our unfeign'd sorrow see;
Oh give us strength to bear our woe,
To bear the loss of Thee!

C H O R U S.

Rise, Rise! &c.

S C E N E II.

M A N T U A.

Enter Romeo.

IF I may trust the flattery of sleep,
  My dreams presage some joyful news at hand :
My bosom's lord sits lightly on his throne,
And all this day, an unaccustom'd spirit
Lifts me above the ground with chearful thoughts.
I dreamt my lady came and found me dead,
And breath'd such life with kisses in my lips,
That I reviv'd and was an Emperor.
Ah me! how sweet is love itself possest,
When but love's shadows are so rich in joy?

Enter Balthazar.

News from *Verona*—How now, *Balthazar?*
Dost thou not bring me Letters from the Friar ?
How doth my lady? is my father well ?
How doth my *Juliet?* that I ask again,
For nothing can be ill, if she be well.

  Bal. Then she is well, and nothing can be ill,
Her body sleeps in *Capulet's* monument,
And her immortal part with angels lives :
I saw her carried to her kindred's vault,
And presently took post to tell it you :
O pardon me for bringing these ill news.

  Rom. Is it even so? then I defy you, stars!——
  Bal. My Lord!

Rom.

Rom. Thou know'ſt my lodging, get me ink and paper,
And hire poſt horſes. I will hence to-night.

Bal. Pardon me, Sir, I dare not leave you thus.
Your looks are pale and wild, and do import
Some miſadventure.

Rom. Go, thou art deceiv'd,
Leave me, and do the thing I bid thee do:
Haſt thou no letters to me from the Friar?

Bal. No, good my Lord.

Rom. No matter: Get thee gone,
And hire thoſe horſes, I'll be with thee ſtraight.
                                        [*Exit* Balthazar.

Well, *Juliet*, I will lie with thee to-night; ——
Let's ſee for means——O miſchief! thou art ſwift
To enter in the thought of deſperate men!
I do remember an Apothecary,
And hereabout he dwells, whom late I noted
In tatter'd weeds, with overwhelming brows,
Culling of ſimples; meager were his looks,
Sharp miſery had worn him to the bones:
And in his needy ſhop a tortoiſe hung,
An alligator ſtuft, and other ſkins
Of ill ſhap'd fiſhes; and about his ſhelves
A beggarly account of empty boxes;
Green earthen pots, bladders, and muſty ſeeds,
Remnants of packthread, and old cakes of roſes
Were thinly ſcatter'd, to make up a ſhew.
Noting his penury, to myſelf I ſaid,
An' if a man did need a poiſon now,
Here lives a caitiff wretch would ſell it him.
Oh this ſame thought did but forerun my need,
As I remember this ſhould be the houſe.
Being holy-day, the beggar's ſhop is ſhut.
What ho! apothecary!

Enter Apothecary.

Ap. Who calls ſo loud?

Rom. Come hither, man; I ſee that thou art poor;
Hold, there are forty ducats, let me have
A dram of poiſon, ſuch ſoon-ſpeeding geer,
As will diſperſe itſelf thro' all the veins,
That the life-weary Taker may ſoon die.

Ap.

Ap. Such mortal drugs I have, but *Mantua*'s law
Is death to any he that utters them.

Rom. Art thou so bare and full of wretchedness,
And fear'st to die ? famine is in thy cheeks,
Need and oppression stare within thine eyes,
Contempt and beggary hang on thy back :
The world is not thy friend, nor the world's law ;
The world affords no law to make thee rich :
Then be not poor, but break it, and take this.

Ap. My poverty, but not my will consents.   [*Exit.*
Rom. I pay thy poverty, and not thy will.
[*Apothecary returns.*
Ap. Put this in any liquid thing you will,
And drink it off, and if you had the strength
Of twenty men it would dispatch you straight.

Rom. There is thy gold, worse poison to mens souls,
Doing more murder in this loathsome world,
Than these poor compounds that thou may'st not sell :
I sell thee poison, thou hast sold me none.
Farewel, buy food, and get thee into flesh.
Come cordial, and not poison, go with me
To *Juliet*'s grave, for there must I use thee.[*Exeunt.*

S C E N E   III.

The Monastery at Verona.

Enter Friar John *to Friar* Lawrence.

John. **H**OLY *Franciscan* Friar! brother ! ho !
Law. This same should be the voice of
Friar *John,*
Welcome from *Mantua*; what says *Romeo* ?
Or if his mind be writ, give me his letter.

John. Going to find a bare-foot brother out,
One of our order to associate me,
Here in this city visiting the sick ;

And

And finding him, the searchers of the town,
(Suspecting that we both were in a house
Where the infectious pestilence did reign,)
Seal'd up the doors, and would not let us forth,
So that my speed to *Mantua* there was staid.

   Law. Who bore my letter then to *Romeo?*

   John. I could not send it; here it is again,
Nor get a messenger to bring it thee,
So fearful were they of infection.

   Law. Unhappy fortune! by my brotherhood,
The letter was not nice, but full of charge,
Of dear import, and the neglecting it
May do much danger. Friar *John*, go hence,
Get me an iron crow, and bring it straight
Unto my cell.

   John. Brother, I'll bring it thee.   [*Exit.*

   Law. Now must I to the monument alone:
Within these three hours will fair *Juliet* wake;
She will beshrew me much that *Romeo*
Hath had no notice of these accidents:
But I will write again to *Mantua*,
And keep her at my cell 'till *Romeo* come.
Poor living coarse, clos'd in a dead man's tomb!   [*Exit.*

S C E N E. IV.

*A Church-yard: In it, a Monument belonging to
the* Capulets.

Enter Paris, *and his Page, with a light.*

Par. GIVE me thy torch, boy; hence, and stand
           aloof.
Yet put it out, for I would not be seen:
Under yond yew-tree lay thee all along,
Placing thy ear close to the hollow ground;

                             So

So shall no foot upon the church-yard tread,
(Being loose, unfirm, with digging up of graves)
But thou shalt hear it : whistle then to me,
As signal that thou hear'st something approach.
Give me those flow'rs. Do as I bid thee ; go.

Page. I am almost afraid to stand alone
Here in the church-yard, yet I will adventure. [*Exit.*

Par. Sweet flow'rs ! with flow'rs thy bridal bed I
    strew ; [*Strewing flowers.*
Fair *Juliet*, that with angels dost remain,
Accept this latest favour at my hand,
That living honour'd thee, and being dead
With fun'ral obsequies adorn thy tomb.
[*The boy whistles.*
—The boy gives warning, something doth approach——
What cursed foot wanders this way to night,
To cross my obsequies ?
What, with a torch ? muffle me, night, a while. [*Paris retires.*

S C E N E V.

Enter Romeo *and* Balthasar *with a light.*

Rom. GIVE me the wrenching iron,
    Hold, take this letter ; early in the morning
See thou deliver it to my lord and father.
Put out the torch, and on thy life I charge thee,
Whate'er thou hear'st or seest, stand all aloof,
And do not interrupt me in my course.
Why I descend into this bed of death,
Is partly to behold my lady's face :
But chiefly to take thence from her dead finger
A precious ring, a ring that I must use
In dear employment ; therefore hence, be gone :
But if thou, jealous, dost return to pry
In what I further shall intend to do,
By heaven I will tear thee joint by joint,

                   And

And ſtrew this hungry church-yard with thy limbs ;
The time and my intents are ſavage-wild,
More fierce and more inexorable far
Than empty tigers, or the roaring ſea.

Bal. I will be gone, Sir, and not trouble you.

Rom. So ſhalt thou win my favour. Take thou that,
Live and be proſp'rous, and farewel, good fellow.

Bal. For all this ſame, I'll hide me near this place ;
His looks I fear, and his intents I doubt.   [*Exit.*

Rom. Thou deteſtable maw, thou womb of death,
Gorg'd with the deareſt morſel of the earth ;
Thus I enforce thy rotten jaws to open.

            [*Breaking open the monument.*

And in deſpight I'll cram thee with more food.

Par. [*Shewing himſelf.*] Stop thy unhallow'd toil, vile
    Montague :
Can vengeance be purſu'd further than death ?
Condemned villain, I do apprehend thee ;
Obey, and go with me, for thou muſt die.

Rom. I muſt indeed, and therefore came I hither——
Good gentle youth, tempt not a deſp'rate man,
Fly hence and leave me :
By heaven I love thee better than myſelf ;
For I come hither arm'd againſt myſelf.

Par. I do defie thy pity and thy counſel,
And apprehend thee for a felon here.

Rom. Wilt thou provoke me? then have at thee, boy.
            [*They fight,* Paris *falls.*

Page. Oh lord, they fight ! I will go call the watch.

Par. Oh I am ſlain ; if thou be merciful,
Open the tomb, lay me with *Juliet.*   [*Dies.*

Rom. In faith, I will : let me peruſe this face——
Mercutio's kinſman ! Noble County *Paris* !
Give me thy hand,
One writ with me in four misfortune's book,
I'll bury thee in a triumphant grave,
For here lies *Juliet*—Oh my love, my wife,
Death that hath ſuckt the honey of thy breath,
Hath had no power yet upon thy beauty :
Thou art not conquer'd, beauty's enſign yet
Is crimſon in thy lips, and in thy cheeks,

                      And

And death's pale flag is not advanced there.
Oh *Juliet*, why art thou yet so fair——here, **here**
Will I set up my everlasting rest;
And shake the yoke of inauspicious stars
From this world-weary flesh.
Come bitter conduct, come unsavoury guide,
Thou desp'rate pilot, now at once run on
The dashing rocks my sea-sick weary bark:
No more—here's to my love—eyes, look your last;
Arms, take your last embrace; and Lips, do you
The doors of breath seal with a righteous kiss.——
Soft——soft——she breathes, and stirs!   [*Juliet wakes.*

　　Jul. Where am I? defend me, powers!
　　Rom. She speaks, she lives; and we shall still be
　　　　bless'd!
My kind propitious stars o'erpay me now
For all my sorrows past—rise, rise my *Juliet*,
And from this cave of death, this house of horror,
Quick let me snatch thee to thy *Romeo*'s arms,
There breathe a vital spirit in thy lips,
And call thee back to life and love!   [*Takes her hand.*

　　Jul. Bless me! how cold it is! who's there!
　　Rom. Thy husband,
It is thy *Romeo*, love; rais'd from despair
To joys unutterable! quit, quit this place,
And let us fly together——   [*Brings her from the tomb.*

　　Jul. Why do you force me so—I'll ne'er consent—
My strength may fail me, but my will's unmov'd,——
I'll not wed *Paris*,—*Romeo* is my husband—
　　Rom. Her senses are unsettl'd—restore 'em, Heav'n!
Romeo is thy husband; I am that *Romeo*,
Nor all th' opposing pow'rs of earth or man,
Can break our bonds, or tear thee from my heart.
　　Jul. I know that voice—Its magic sweetness wakes
My tranced soul——I now remember well
Each circumstance——Oh my lord, my *Romeo*!
Had'st thou not come, sure I had slept for ever;
But there's a sovereign charm in thy embraces
That can revive the dead——Oh honest *Friar*!——

　　　　　　　　　　　　　　　　　　　　Dost

Doſt thou avoid me, *Romeo ?* let me touch
Thy hand, and taſte the cordial of thy lips——
You fright me—ſpeak·—Oh let me hear ſome voice
Beſides my own in this drear vault of death,
Or I ſhall faint——ſupport me——

    Rom. Oh I cannot,
I have no ſtrength, but want thy feeble aid,
Cruel poiſon !

    Jul. Poiſon ! what means my lord ; thy trembling
        voice !
Pale lips ! and ſwimming eyes ! death's in thy face !

    Rom. It is indeed—— I ſtruggle with him now——
The tranſports that I felt, to hear thee ſpeak,
And ſee thy op'ning eyes, ſtopt for a moment
His impetuous courſe, and all my mind
Was happineſs and thee ; but now the poiſon
Ruſhes thro' my veins—— I've not time to tell——
Fate brought me to this place—to take a laſt,
Laſt farewel of my love and with thee die.

    Jul. Die ! was the *Friar* falſe !

    Rom. I know not that——
I thought thee dead ; diſtracted at the ſight,
(Fatal ſpeed) drank poiſon, kiſs'd thy cold lips,
And found within thy arms a precious grave——
But in that moment——Oh——

    Jul. And did I wake for this !

    Rom. My powers are blaſted,
'Twixt death and love I'm torn—I am diſtracted !
But death's ſtrongeſt——and muſt I leave thee, *Juliet !*
Oh cruel curſed fate ! in ſight of heav'n——

    Jul. Thou rav'ſt——lean on my breaſt ——

    Rom. Fathers have flinty hearts, no tears can melt
    'em.
Nature pleads in vain——Children muſt be wretched—

    Jul. Oh my breaking heart——

    Rom. She is my wife—our hearts are twin'd together—
Capulet, forbear —*Paris,* looſe your hold——
Pull not our heart-ſtrings thus——they crack——they
    break——

                    Oh

Oh *Juliet!* *Juliet!* [*Dies.*

Jul. Stay, ſtay, for me, *Romeo*——
A moment ſtay ; fate marries us in death,
And we are *one*— no pow'r ſhall part us.
[*Faints on* Romeo's *body.*

Enter Friar Lawrence, *with lanthorn, crow and ſpade.*

Fri. St. *Francis* be my ſpeed ! how oft to-night,
Have my old feet ſtumbled at graves ! who's there,
Alack, alack ! what blood is this which ſtains
The ſtony entrance of this ſepulchre !

Jul. Who's there !

Fri. Ah *Juliet* awake, and *Romeo* dead !
And *Paris* too — Oh what an unkind hour
Is guilty of this lamentable chance !

Jul. Here he is ſtill, and I will hold him faſt,
They ſhall not tear him from me ——

Fri. Patience, Lady——

Jul. Who is that ! Oh thou curſed *Friar !* **patience !**
Talk'ſt thou of patience to a wretch like me !

Fri. O fatal error ! riſe, thou fair diſtreſt,
And fly this ſcene of death !

Jul. Come thou not near me,
Or this dagger ſhall quit my *Romeo's* death.
[*Draws a dagger.*

Fri. I wonder not thy griefs have made thee deſp'rate.
What noiſe without ? ſweet *Juliet*, let us fly——
A greater pow'r than we can contradict,
Hath thwarted our intents ——come, haſte away.
I will diſpoſe thee, moſt unhappy lady,
Amongſt a ſiſterhood of holy nuns :
Stay not to queſtion——for the watch is coming,
Come, go good *Juliet*——I dare no longer ſtay. [*Exit.*

Jul. Go, get thee hence, I will not away——
What's here ! a phial——*Romeo's* timeleſs end.
O churl drink all, and leave no friendly drop
To help me after——I will kiſs thy lips,
Haply ſome poiſon yet doth hang on them——
[*Kiſſes him.*

[Watch

[Watch *and* Page *within.*]

Watch. Lead, boy, which way ——
Jul. Noiſe again!
Then I'll be brief——Oh happy dagger!
This is thy ſheath, there reſt and let me die.
[*Kills herſelf.*

Boy. This is the place——my liege.

Enter Prince, &c.

Prin. What miſadventure is ſo early up,
That calls our perſon from its morning's reſt?

Enter Capulet.

Cap. What ſhould it be that they ſo ſhriek abroad!
The people in the ſtreet cry *Romeo*,
Some *Juliet* and ſome *Paris* ; and all run
With open outcry tow'rd our monument.
Prin. What fear is this which ſtartles in your ears?
Watch. Sov'reign, here lies the County *Paris* ſlain,
And *Romeo* dead——*Juliet* thought dead before
Is warm and newly kill'd——
Cap. Oh me, this ſight of death is as a bell,
That warns my old age to a ſepulchre.

Enter Mountague.

Prin. Come *Mountague*, for thou art early up,
To ſee thy ſon and heir now early fall'n——
Moun. Alas my liege my wife is dead to night,
Grief of my ſon's exile hath ſtop'd her breath :
What farther woe conſpires againſt my age !
Prin. Look there—— and ſee——
Moun. Oh thou untaught, what manners is in this,
To preſs before thy father to a grave !
Prin. Seal up the mouth of outrage for a while
Till we can clear theſe ambiguities,
And know their ſpring and head—— mean time forbear
And let miſchance be ſlave to patience :
Bring forth the parties of ſuſpicion.

Fri.